THE
ROBERT LOUIS STEVENSON
TRAIL

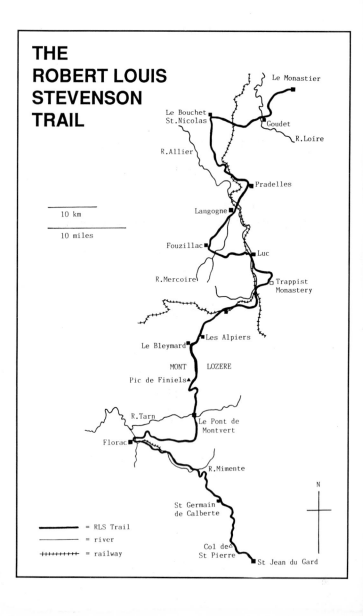

THE ROBERT LOUIS STEVENSON TRAIL

Le Monastier

Le Bouchet St.Nicolas

Goudet

R.Loire

R.Allier

Pradelles

Langogne

Fouzillac

Luc

R.Mercoire

Trappist Monastery

Le Bleymard

Les Alpiers

MONT   LOZERE

Pic de Finiels

R.Tarn

Le Pont de Montvert

Florac

R.Mimente

St Germain de Calberte

Col de St Pierre

St Jean du Gard

10 km

10 miles

N

━━━━ = RLS Trail
───── = river
++++++++ = railway

THE
ROBERT LOUIS STEVENSON
TRAIL

A Walking Tour in the
Velay and Cévennes, Southern France

by

Alan Castle

This guidebook is produced
with the approval and assistance of the
Club Cévenol

CICERONE PRESS
Milnthorpe, Cumbria

ACKNOWLEDGEMENTS

I am indebted to Madame Pat Valette of the Club Cévenol for advice, local information and encouragement. Her knowledge of the Cévennes and her many contacts within France have greatly facilitated the compilation of this guidebook. I am also most grateful to Pat and Pierre Valette for their critical reading of the manuscript.

Thanks must also go to Mr Robin Hill of the RLS Society in Edinburgh for background information, particularly on the centenary celebrations in 1978, and for providing encouragement and a list of further contacts. One of these was Miss Ellen Shaffer of the Silverado Museum in California, USA, to whom I am most grateful for archive material.

I would also thank Laurie Lowe for checking various details of the route.

Thanks are extended to Andrée Cain for help with the French language and to Joan Newman who typed part of the manuscript. As always I am grateful to my wife for her support, advice and encouragement.

The author wishes to thank Club Cévenol, Mainstream Publishing (Edinburgh) and Gordon Golding for permission to quote from *The Cévennes Journal*.

For my part, I travel not to go anywhere, but to go.
I travel for travel's sake.
The great affair is to move.

R.L.Stevenson
Travels with a Donkey, 1879

Dedicated to all who would follow
in the footsteps of Stevenson and Modestine

CONTENTS

GUIDE

INTRODUCTION

THE ROBERT LOUIS STEVENSON TRAIL

The Robert Louis Stevenson Trail is a linear long distance walk through the Velay, Gévaudan and Cévennes regions of southern France. It follows closely, but not exactly, the route taken by the writer R.L. Stevenson, accompanied by his donkey, Modestine, during the autumn of 1878 and later recounted in his first successful book, *Travels with a Donkey in the Cévennes* (1879). The trail meanders south for some 140 miles (225km) from Le Monastier-sur-Gazeille near Le Puy in the Velay, across the Cévennes mountains to finish at St Jean du Gard, west of Alès. In so doing it crosses some of the finest and most remote country in rural France and visits numerous towns and villages of historical importance, including Pradelles, Le Pont de Montvert and Florac. The latter sections of the trail pass through the land of the Camisards, an area ravaged by nearly one hundred years of religious war between the local Protestants and their Catholic rulers.

The trail is not, as Stevenson suggests, wholly within the Cévennes. The walk starts in the Velay in which it remains until Langogne where it enters the ancient district of Gévaudan, bordering on Vivarais, the modern Ardèche. The Cévennes is not actually encountered until Mont Lozère, just after the half-way mark. The trail passes through three modern départements: the Haute-Loire until just before Langogne, Lozère for much of the remainder of the journey and Gard for the last few miles into St Jean du Gard. The Haute-Loire belongs to the Auvergne Region, whilst Lozère and Gard form part of the Region of Languedoc-Roussillon.

The trail follows footpaths, ancient drove roads or *drailles*, bridleways and a number of quiet roads. It is not a particularly demanding walk in either terrain or distance, fitting conveniently into a fortnight's holiday, allowing time at the beginning and end of the walk, as well as at a number of points in between, for sightseeing. It is suitable as a first walking holiday for those with little or no experience of long distance walking, although it would pay to reach some level of fitness before setting out. The second half of the walk in the Cévennes is noticeably more hilly than the first stages in the Velay and Gévaudan, but by then the wayfarer should be 'trail fit' taking the relatively modest ascents and descents in his or her stride. It is difficult to compare the 'grade' of this walk with any in the UK as the landscape is so totally different from any encountered in the British Isles, and there are other factors to consider, such as the heat of the summer sun in these southerly latitudes. That being stated, the RLS Trail can be likened in severity more to the South Downs Way than to the Pennine Way. The comparison ends there!

An inspection of the route followed by Stevenson (affectionately known as RLS) will soon reveal that the writer did not take a direct line through these mountains, the path wandering several times to the west and east on its journey south. There are a number of possible reasons for this meandering route. Firstly, it seems likely that Stevenson was not the best of navigators and furthermore the maps he carried may not have been very reliable (they almost certainly did not show the new roads that were being built at the time). Many of the people that he encountered were unwilling or unable to direct him to his desired destination, and on at least one occasion (at Fouzillic/Fouzillac) he became hopelessly lost. Secondly, his inquisitive, educated mind encouraged him to seek out places of interest some distance from the natural line of the route. This was almost certainly the reason for his detour to the west on his first day as he sought, but never found, the volcanic Lac du Bouchet. Thirdly, there were relatively few places on his journey where RLS could re-stock his and Modestine's food supplies. This may well have been the reason for the lengthy loop to Florac down the Tarn valley and back up the valley of the Mimente. Lastly, the philosophy of Stevenson must be remembered - he *"travelled not to go anywhere, but to go"*.

The RLS Trail as described in this guidebook does not follow exactly in the footsteps of Stevenson and Modestine. Several of the paths and tracks used by RLS have now been metalled and incorporated into the current road network. The modern route was designed to provide as scenic a walk as possible, avoiding busy roads and making use of the excellent system of long distance paths (*Grandes Randonnées*, q.v) available in France. Nevertheless, the itinerary described herein visits all of the principal towns and villages, with the exception of those in the Tarn valley between Le Pont de Montvert and Florac, mentioned by RLS. The person responsible for the line of the modern trail, based on Stevenson's few actual references, was M. Raymond Senn of the Mendois Hikers, who coordinated a team of local workers to iron out the problems of their allotted sections. The route uses some roads but these are nearly all minor ones, where the volume of traffic, even in the summer holiday season, is very low.

ROBERT LOUIS STEVENSON

Robert Louis Stevenson, the great nineteenth century writer and novelist, was born at 8 Howard Place in Edinburgh on November 13, 1850. A Scot, the only child of Thomas and Margaret Stevenson, he was christened Robert Lewis Balfour Stevenson. The 'Lewis' was later changed to the French spelling, although the pronunciation of the final 's' was retained all his life. It was this name, Louis, by which he was known to family and friends.

RLS was a sickly child whose schooling was often interrupted by chronic respiratory illnesses. In attempts to alleviate the symptoms he was sent to spend extended periods in the warmer parts of Europe, principally France, where he often stayed with his mother in Menton on the Côte d'Azur. An imaginative boy, he spent long periods alone as a child, developing a taste for literature from an early age and a desire to become a writer. His first attempts at writing were made at the age of sixteen.

Stevenson came from a family of eminent engineers: his grandfather, Robert, was a celebrated civil engineer whilst his father was appointed Inspector of Lighthouses in Scotland. Louis was expected to follow in his father's footsteps and to this end was sent up to Edinburgh University in 1867 to read engineering. However, he had no interest in the subject and before qualifying he changed to study law, much to the bitter disappointment of his father. He eventually qualified as a Scottish advocate (the equivalent of a barrister) but he never practised.

His desire to write continued into his young adult life, despite his father's belief that writing was not a suitable career. In 1873 he met Mrs Frances Sitwell, a beautiful and intellectual woman who became his confidante, introducing him to Sidney Colvin, Slade Professor of Fine Art at Cambridge. Colvin was to remain a lifelong friend, critic and sponsor of RLS (see the dedication and letter to Sidney Colvin that acts as a preface to *Travels with a Donkey*) and it was Colvin who helped Stevenson to get many of his early works published in a number of literary magazines.

His meagre earnings from these early writings, together with small allowances from his father, enabled him to spend much of the period between 1873 and 1879, during his mid-twenties, in France. He became a 'Bohemian' during this period, wearing his hair long and frequenting a number of French art colonies in and around Paris, a life he was introduced to by his cousin, a painter.

In 1876 Stevenson undertook a short adventure with his friend Sir Walter Simpson, canoeing along the rivers and canals of France and Belgium. His exploits were later assembled into his first published book, *An Inland Voyage* (1878).

On his return to the art colony in Grez, Stevenson met and fell deeply in love with an American woman ten years his senior, Mrs Frances (Fanny or 'F') Matilda Osbourne, who was separated from her husband and living with her two children in Europe. In 1878 Fanny Osbourne returned to California in the pursuit of a divorce, leaving Stevenson distraught in France. Partly to console himself for this (temporary) loss of Fanny and partly to provide material for a second book, RLS left for the Auvergne and Cévennes, an area hitherto unknown to him. He was then twenty-seven years old. After spending a month in Le Monastier he set out on Sunday September 22, accompanied by his newly acquired donkey, Modestine, on his now famous journey on foot through the Velay, Gévaudan and Cévennes.

On his return to Scotland, Stevenson adapted the journal that he had kept whilst on the walk and presented it for publication as *Travels with a Donkey in the Cévennes*. It was published the following year, 1879, and was to become his first successful book. In the same year he followed Mrs Osbourne to California where he spent the winter desperately short of money. Fanny eventually obtained a divorce and on May 19, 1880, she and Stevenson, then thirty-one years of age, were married.

Fanny was to devote the next fourteen years of her life to caring for her often ill husband. In the same year as their marriage Stevenson was diagnosed as suffering from tuberculosis. Nevertheless, the sunshine and warmth of California were beneficial to his health and it was during this period that he was at his most prolific and successful as a writer, producing the classics *Treasure Island* (1883), *A Child's Garden of Verses* (1885), *Dr Jekyll and Mr Hyde* (1886) and *Kidnapped* (1886). Periods of calm and happiness were interspersed with bouts of illness which he tried to relieve with trips to Switzerland, the south of France and Bournemouth. From 1887-8 he stayed at Saranac Lake, New York State where he was (wrongly) pronounced cured.

In the search for new writing material and on receipt of a huge advance from his publisher, Stevenson chartered a yacht to the South Pacific accompanied by Fanny and his mother and stepson. They spent a year travelling visiting the Marquesas, Tahiti, Hawaii, Micronesia and Australia. After this period RLS bought a tropical estate of 400 acres on the island of Upolu in Samoa in 1890. Here at Vailima (Five Streams) he built a large house in which he entertained native dignitaries and visiting westerners. He settled down to a new life in a climate that was to his liking, becoming involved in local politics and writing some of his best works. He was part way through *The Weir of Hermiston* (published posthumously in 1896) when he died unexpectedly, shortly after a massive cerebral haemorrhage on December 3, 1894. The natives buried him in Samoa on the summit of Mount Pala. His famous requiem is inscribed (incorrectly) on the tomb:

> *Here he lies where he longed to be;*
> *Home is the sailor, home from sea,*
> *And the hunter home from the hill.*

TRAVELS WITH A DONKEY IN THE CEVENNES

Robert Louis Stevenson's journey through the Velay, Gévaudan and Cévennes began on Sunday September 22, 1878 and lasted for just twelve days, terminating at St Jean du Gard on Thursday October 3. This walking tour was quite short and modest in nature and hardly ranks in the long catalogue of adventurous journeys undertaken on foot by Victorian travellers. Nevertheless, the book *Travels with a Donkey in the Cévennes* describing his adventures is a delightful minor classic, much read and still in publication today. The journey has captured the imagination of both walkers and lovers of literature alike ever since the publication of the book, and the route Stevenson pursued through this attractive, ancient landscape of southern France is followed faithfully by many present day ramblers. An outline of his exploits on the trail is given in the various Travels with a Donkey sections in the guide part of this book. Details of his itinerary are provided in Appendix Three.

RLS had resided in Le Monastier-sur-Gazeille for several weeks prior to embarking on his trek and it was in this town that he purchased the female donkey, Modestine, which was to accompany him on his travels. He must have aroused considerable curiosity amongst the local inhabitants - *"A traveller of my sort was a thing hitherto unheard of in that district."*

Certain writers and poets have been renowned for their walking prowess. For example, William Wordsworth was an ardent tramper of the Lakeland fells and valleys; it has been estimated that during his long life he walked around 180,000 miles for pleasure. Hilaire Belloc and William Hazlitt were other well-known ramblers. However, RLS cannot be placed in this category; he undertook relatively few walking excursions and in fact no other extended travels on foot were recorded after his sojourn in the Cévennes. Stevenson was first and foremost a writer and his major reason for undertaking the Cévennes trip was to obtain material for publication. Nevertheless, he had written an essay during this period of his life on the merits and pleasures of walking. In this he advised solitude on a walking tour, suggesting that only when alone can the experience of being out in the countryside be fully appreciated. Solitary tramping is perhaps less popular today; indeed some authorities frown upon it from a safety point of view, although it was strongly advocated by the modern guru of hill walking, Alfred Wainwright.

Stevenson chose to tour the Cévennes without a human companion, perhaps because he wanted time to consider his entanglement with Fanny Osbourne, but more probably because he saw his task as a job of work, amassing information and experiences that he could convert into a book on his return home. He needed time to write his daily journal and indeed this was the main reason for several late daily starts. Of the twelve days on the trail, five were really only 'half-day' walks. His late starts sometimes resulted in his arriving at his destination in the dark, for example at St Germain-de-Calberte and on the last day in St Jean-du-Gard. The original and complete notebook compiled by RLS whilst on his Cévennes journey was re-discovered in the 1970s by an American relative of a *Club Cévenol* member in Yale University Library in the USA, and was published in French by *Club Cévenol* (q.v.) and in English by Mainstream Publishing (Edinburgh) in 1978 under the title *The Cévennes Journal* (see Bibliography).

The aspect that distinguishes Stevenson's journey through the Cévennes from all other well known accounts of pedestrian wanderings is the presence of the *"diminutive she-ass"*, Modestine. Not only does the donkey provide an admirable title for his subsequent book, but it forms the central character of the tale, providing considerable quantity of literary copy. RLS probably did not have this in mind when he acquired the donkey, which he judged necessary for carrying the voluminous and heavy equipment he considered essential for camping out in the wild. From a walker's point of view, to take a donkey on such a trip, particularly a female animal on heat, was a mistake, requiring a great deal of nervous and physical energy on the part of Stevenson to persuade the animal to progress at a reasonable pace. But from a literary point of view, and this was how his adventure was later to be assessed, the inclusion of Modestine was a great success. *Travels with a Donkey in the Cévennes*, published a year after his journey would no doubt have suffered a very different fate had RLS chosen to go on his travels completely alone. As it is, the book was his first real success, launching him on a career which was to produce some of the classics of the English language. Whether *Travels with a Donkey* would be read so avidly today and the trail followed by so many modern pilgrims, if R.L. Stevenson had not gone on to achieve such literary fame, is a matter for conjecture.

To walk the RLS Trail today is perhaps at times a rather eerie experience, almost like following in the footsteps of a ghost. When walking the route one may receive a strong feeling of one's own mortality. The places in this quiet region of France are much the same today as they were in the 1870s, but the people Stevenson describes, children and all, have long since departed this life. And so it will be in the next 110 years' time.

THE MASSIF CENTRAL. VELAY, GEVAUDAN AND VIVARAIS

The first half of the RLS Trail passes through the areas known as the Velay and Gévaudan, and skirts the ancient region of Vivarais. Part of the Auvergne, much of this land is contained within the modern Ardèche. These various regions, as well as the Cévennes itself, are all part of the high mountainous plateau of southern central France known as the Massif Central. This largely remote area of some 36,000 sq.miles (93,000 sq.km) in extent, is a major source of hydro-electric power for France. The only major city in the region is Clermont-Ferrand (population 155,000), industrial in nature, situated to the north of the area covered by this guidebook. Much of the land in the Massif Central is about 1,000m (3,278ft) in altitude, the highest point being the Puy de Sancy at 1,885m (6,180ft) above Le Mont-Dore to the south-west of Clermont-Ferrand. The notorious *'Mistral'* wind of the eastern Mediterranean originates in the cold air above the Massif Central.

It is an old saying in this region of France that the Auvergne is a 'gift of its volcanoes'. The landscape as seen today with its many pointed *puys* and *sucs* is the product of vigorous volcanic activity stretching over a vast period of time. Much of the land was shaped by gigantic earth movements around thirty-five million years ago when the African plate collided with Europe to form the Alps. Many other volcanoes in the Auvergne are of much more recent origin; considerable volcanic activity took place in the area around 8000BC. There are many thousands of extinct volcanoes in the Auvergne often strung out across the landscape as chains of puys. The most well known areas are the Puys de Dôme and Mont-Dore to the west and south-west of Clermont-Ferrand, Cantal to the west of St-Flour and the Velay around Le Puy. This region of France holds many attractions for the walker and further exploration on foot is highly recommended.

The Velay, with its capital Le Puy, is one of the best known of the volcanic regions of the Auvergne. Le Puy itself is a very popular tourist centre, rightly so for it has much to offer the discerning visitor. The source of one of France's most attractive and well known rivers, the Loire, is to be found in the Velay, on the slopes of Le Gerbier de Jonc 1,551m (5,085ft) to the south-west of Le Puy. The River Loire penetrates the heart of the Velay, giving its name to the modern département of the Haute-Loire. Near to Le Gerbier de Jonc is the watershed between the Atlantic and Mediterranean. Not far away lies Mont Mézenc at 1,753m (5,747ft) the highest peak in the Velay. The region can be more fully explored on foot by following the GR40, the circular Tour of the Velay (see Bibliography).

The Velay is left behind and the area known as Gévaudan entered at Langogne. This remote, sparsely populated land, home of the eighteenth century Beast of Gévaudan, borders on another ancient region of France, the Vivarais. This little known area dates back to before the French Revolution at the time of the *Ancien Régime*. There are several GR trails throughout Vivarais, perhaps the most rewarding being the Tour of the High-Vivarais, the GR420, a circular route of some 125 miles (201km).

There are many *drailles* or drove roads in this part of France. These were used for centuries for the 'transhumance', the system of moving animals from lower to upper pastures for the summer months. Several hundred sheep, with an ass or two and a few goats, would be herded up to the hills in April by two or three shepherds who would remain in the high pastures with their flock until the return to the lower valleys in September, October, or even November if the weather held. This system continued until the late 1970s, but nowadays most of the movement of stock takes place along the main roads in lorries. The traditional ways of this ancient land are fast disappearing with the 'progress' of the late twentieth century. Nevertheless the *drailles* make excellent cross-country walking tracks and several have been incorporated into the RLS Trail and the various GR routes in the area.

THE CEVENNES. LE PARC NATIONAL DES CEVENNES

The Cévennes is a rugged mountainous region forming the south-eastern edge of the Massif Central. The northern boundary of the Cévennes is generally taken to be the high tableland of Mont Lozère, the summit of which at 1,699m (5,570ft) is its highest point. The region extends southwards to Mont Aigoual 1,565m (5,130ft) a peak of granite and schist which, after Mont Lozère, is the best known mountain in the area. The Cévennes is bordered by the Vivarais and the depopulated Margeride to the north, the limestone *causses* to the south and west, and to the east lies Alès, the largest town in the region. It is a land of wooded hillsides, mountains and rushing streams; there are many tributaries of the River Gardon forming deep, steep-sided valleys. The River Tarn rises in the Cévennes and flows through Florac and on for 220 miles (354 kilometres) to join the River Garonne. It is most well known for its spectacular gorges found to the west of Florac.

The Protestant country of the Cévennes was witness to many atrocities during the Camisard's Revolt in the eighteenth century (see Le Pont de Montvert - Day 8). The modern day Cévenols, although greatly depleted in numbers, are rightly proud of their fine, rugged landscape and their ancient traditions. In the past the people lived largely on chestnuts, olives and vines. Today the population has a high percentage of elderly people as more and more youngsters have moved to the towns in search of employment. Most Cévenols work on the land or in the tourist industry.

The Cévennes National Park, the second largest of the six national parks in France, covers an area of 91,416 hectares (225,889 acres). The park was created in 1970 to protect the landscape and curb the commercial exploitation of the region. There are restrictions on hunting and on the use of tents and caravans within the park boundaries. Planning permission is required for any new building and for the renovation of old buildings in an attempt to retain the traditional styles of architecture characteristic of the region. The RLS Trail enters the park on Mont Lozère (Day 8) and much of the remainder of the walk lies within its boundaries. Since 1984 Le Parc National des Cévennes has been twinned with Le Parc National du Saguenay in Quebec, Canada.

There is much to please the naturalist in the Velay and Cévennes. The woodland is a mixture of deciduous trees and conifers. Oak, beech and chestnut are the predominant trees, the air often being scented during the summer months with honeysuckle and gorse. There is an abundance of wild flowers particularly during the springtime. A large variety of wild mushrooms will be found but great care should be exercised as several are highly toxic. The area is rich in wildlife, animals and birds suffering relatively little from the activities of man. There are buzzards, kestrels and kites, and with luck even eagles may be spotted. Wild boar are said to roam the woods, but a sighting would be an extremely rare occurrence. Even the most unobservant walker will be aware of the insect life, particularly the stridulation of the cicadas during the hot summer months, the noise of which can be remarkably loud at times.

CLIMATE - WHEN TO GO

In general terms, summers in the Massif Central tend to be hot and relatively dry, whilst winters are often cold with heavy snow falls.

In theory at least, the RLS Trail could be walked at any time of the year, although during the winter months very low temperatures coupled with snow and ice would call for considerable experience, particularly on the steeper sections on the southern half of the route. Moreover, hotel and other accommodation would probably pose quite a problem during the winter, except in the skiing areas of the Cévennes. Most people therefore would want to consider only spring, summer or autumn to walk the trail. The summer is undoubtedly the most popular season, although it does have some disadvantages. Firstly, it can become intensely hot during the daytime in July and August. Care must be taken to avoid sunstroke and dehydration. Secondly, finding accommodation for each night will be more of a problem in summer than in early or late season (see 'Hotel Accommodation' and 'Camping').

The flowers and general freshness of springtime can be recommended, as too can the autumn when the golden-brown tints of the turning leaves can be particularly beautiful. The temperature can, however, be quite low both early and late in the year and there can be fairly drastic changes in weather conditions. Much of the trail lies at or above the 1,000m (3,278ft) contour and so it is not surprising that temperatures can often drop rapidly. Remember that Stevenson experienced cold and unpleasant weather on the first part of his journey in late September. Violent thunderstorms, often with little warning of their approach, are not uncommon at any time of the year, particularly after the heat of a summer afternoon.

TRAVELLING TO AND FROM THE RLS TRAIL

There are four possible modes of travel to the Velay and Cévennes from Britain: air, train, coach and private transport. Note that any timetable information given is liable to change. When consulting timetables remember that France is one hour ahead of Britain for most of the year (liable to change).

Air

There are three destinations worthy of consideration. British Airways and Air France are the principal carriers. *AIR CANADA*

Lyon

There is a direct daily service from London Heathrow to Lyon (flight time approximately one and a half hours) with connecting flights from other major British airports to Heathrow. A bus service operates between the airport and Lyon city centre (bus departs approximately every twenty to thirty minutes all day Monday to Friday).

A train can then be taken from Lyon-Perrache to Le Puy (about three trains per day; journey time approximately two and a half hours) for the start of the holiday. At the end of the trail take a bus from St Jean-du-Gard to Alès where a train may be taken to Nîmes and then up the Rhône Valley to Lyon for the flight home.

Clermont-Ferrand

There are daily flights from London Heathrow (limited service on Saturdays) to Clermont-Ferrand via Paris (journey times between three and a half to five hours). The disadvantage is that the flights from London use Paris Charles de Gaulle Airport, whereas the connecting flight to Clermont Ferrand leaves from Paris Orly Airport. A shuttle bus service operates between Charles de Gaulle airport and Orly.

From Clermont Ferrand a train or train and bus may be taken to Le Puy (journey time about one and a quarter hours). At the end of the holiday a mainline train (the Paris-Marseille line) runs several times a day between Alès and Clermont Ferrand, via Langogne (journey time approximately four and a half hours).

Paris

Several flights per day operate between London (Heathrow and Gatwick) and Paris (Charles de Gaulle). Flying time is approximately one hour. Scheduled services also operate from Birmingham, Glasgow and Manchester. Charles de Gaulle International Airport is approximately fifteen miles from Paris city centre (journey time approximately forty-five minutes). There are three possible modes of transport between airport and city: Air France bus, Roissy Rail train and taxi.

Once in Paris the TGV (express train) can be taken to Lyon-Part-Dieu (journey time approximately two hours) and another train from Lyon to Le Puy (see under train below). The return journey to Paris from Alès can also be made via Lyon (see above under 'Lyon').

Train

French Railways or SNCF (Société Nationale de Chemins de Fer) offer a first rate service throughout the country. Trains are generally fast, punctual, clean, comfortable and not overly priced. The journeys from Britain to Le Puy and from the Cévennes back to Britain are both via Paris, and so there are opportunities to spend a day or longer in the capital, if desired, before continuing to Le Puy or returning home.

There are two principal ways in which the train can be used to travel to and from the RLS Trail:

1. *Train and cross-Channel ferry to Paris, followed by train to Le Puy. Return by train from Alès via Paris.*
It is possible to reach Le Puy from London in about fourteen to eighteen hours using train and cross-Channel ferry. The journey can be considered in three stages:

a) *London to Paris*
There are several trains between London and Paris operating daily during the day and night. There are two principal routes:

   i) London Victoria -> Dover or Folkestone -> Calais or Boulogne -> Amiens -> Paris Gare du Nord
      (Journey time approximately seven hours)
   ii) London Victoria -> Newhaven -> Dieppe -> Rouen -> Paris Gare Saint Lazare (journey time approximately nine hours)

Route (ii) involves a longer Channel crossing (about three and three-quarter hours) than Route (i) (about one and three-quarter hours). There is also a nightly service from London Waterloo to Paris via Portsmouth and Le Havre (journey time approximately ten hours). Note that cut-price fares sometimes operate between London and Paris, particularly on night sailings. If travelling from Newhaven or Dover on a night ferry check first whether a cheaper fare is available from London. If making independent travel arrangements to Dover or Newhaven, it is sometimes cheaper to purchase a London to Paris ticket and discard the first part of the ticket to the Channel port. The same applies for a journey from Paris to Newhaven or Dover. However, things often change and so check first before buying a ticket.

From 1994, of course, it will be possible to travel all the way from London to Paris by train, via the Channel Tunnel.

b) *Across Paris*

Trains from Britain arrive in Paris at either Gare Saint-Lazare or Gare du Nord. It will be necessary to cross Paris to the Gare de Lyon for trains to Le Puy. The easiest way of travelling across the capital (other than by taxi) is to make use of the Metro (underground) system. Simply ask for one ticket. There is no need to state the station to which one is travelling as there is a fixed price whatever the destination. Note that if spending some time in Paris it is more economical to buy a *carnet* of ten Metro tickets. Crossing Paris can be somewhat of a hassle, particularly if unsure of the system, and so it is a good idea to write down the following brief instructions on a small piece of paper or card that can be kept in the pocket and discarded later. Armed with this it will be unnecessary to consult Metro maps at stations.

1. From Gare du Nord to Gare de Lyon. Line five (Direction Place d'Italie) to Bastille (seven stops). Change to line one (Direction Château de Vincennes) to Gare de Lyon (one stop).

2. From Gare Saint Lazare to Gare de Lyon. Line twelve (Direction Mairie d'Issy) to Concorde (two stops). Change to line one (Direction Château de Vincennes) to Gare de Lyon (eight stops).

On the return journey:

1. From Gare de Lyon to Gare du Nord. Line one (Direction

Pont de Neuilly) to Bastille (one stop). Change to line five (Direction Bobigny-Pablo-Picasso) to Gare du Nord (seven stops).

2. From Gare de Lyon to Gare Saint Lazare. Line one (Direction Pont de Neuilly) to Concorde (eight stops). Change to line twelve (Direction Porte de la Chapelle) to Gare Saint Lazare (two stops).

The journey time is approximately half an hour, although it is wise to allow at least an hour (preferably two) between main line trains arriving from London and departing to Le Puy. Small maps of the Metro system (and also the bus and RER services) can be obtained free of charge at Metro stations. Ask for a 'Petit Plan de Paris'.

Note that a few main line trains (SNCF) operate between Gare du Nord and the Gare de Lyon. These are not often convenient.

c. *Paris to Le Puy. Return from Alès via Paris*
There are two train routes to Le Puy from Paris.

i) *Via Lyon.* This makes use of the incredibly fast and comfortable TGV (see below) service between Paris Gare de Lyon and Lyon-Part-Dieu. The journey time between Paris and Lyon is only two hours. Several trains operate each day. The second stage of the journey is from Lyon-Perrache to Le Puy via St-Etienne (journey time approximately two and a half hours; about three trains per day). Note that Lyon has two main line stations, Part-Dieu and Perrache. Several main line trains run between the two stations. Small blue timetables ('horaires') can be obtained at mainline stations (eg. at Paris Gare de Lyon) giving information on the current trains operating between Paris and Le Puy. Timetable No.529A is the relevant sheet.

ii) *Via Clermont-Ferrand.* Several express trains (Corail) operate daily between Paris Gare de Lyon and Clermont Ferrand. The journey time is approximately four hours. The relevant small blue timetable is sheet No.511. Train services operate between Clermont-Ferrand and Le Puy via Issoire, Arvant, Brioude and St Georges d'Aurac. Sometimes a connecting SNCF bus is necessary between St Georges d'Aurac and Le Puy.

The return home by train is made from Alès, reached by bus from St Jean du Gard. Several express trains, including a night service, operate between Alès and Paris Gare de Lyon via Langogne, Clermont-Ferrand and Nevers. Journey time is approximately eight and a half hours. The relevant small blue timetable is sheet No.510 (Paris-Marseille via Clermont-Ferrand).

2. *Airplane to/from Paris and train from Paris to Le Puy and back to Paris from Alès.*

This is possibly the best combination of air and train travel. The somewhat lengthy and unpleasant Channel crossing is avoided and the trains from and back to Paris are fast and convenient. Details of the two stages of the journey have been given in the relevant sections above. Air France and SNCF sometimes offer combined air and rail tickets at very reasonable prices, ie. air to Paris and train from there to one's destination.

General Information about Rail Travel in France

a) *Booking*

Travel centres in major British Rail stations in most large cities in the UK can supply timetable and price information and can also book tickets and make seat and couchette reservations. A seat/couchette reservation is advisable if travelling during the peak holiday season (particularly at weekends) but note that SNCF reservations will only be accepted within two months of travel date. Note that it is not absolutely necessary to book tickets in Britain for the whole journey eg. if staying for a short while in Paris before travelling to Le Puy, more flexibility will be available if a ticket to Le Puy is purchased at the Gare de Lyon prior to departure. The same is true for the return journey. Buying a train ticket at a railway station in France is no more difficult than in Britain. However, there are two problems with this option, viz. all the seats may already have been booked (this is a particular problem in main season at weekends) and if one's French is poor then the wrong ticket may be bought! A ticket purchased in Britain is valid for two months from the date of outward travel. A ticket bought at a railway station in France is valid for two months from the date of purchase. Tickets can be used on any trains, although on certain services (see below) a supplement may be payable. Seat and couchette reservations are extra (second class couchette was 77FF in 1990).

b) *Types of Trains*

The French are justly proud of their train service and boast that 1,400 express trains run every day throughout France. Most of the services of interest to those wishing to reach the Velay and Cévennes use express trains and many of these are special trains such as the air-conditioned Corail Trains. The pride of French Railways is the TGV (*train à grand vitesse*) which routinely travels up to 168mph. A world record of over 350mph was set in the spring of 1990 (not on a passenger train!). A supplement is payable on all TGV services. The main one of interest is that between Paris and Lyons.

All express trains have some form of catering, from a simple 'mini-bar' pushed by an attendant passing through a train, to a lavish restaurant car as on TGVs.

Couchettes are equipped with bed linen, pillows and blankets. There are six berths per compartment in second class and four berths per compartment in first class.

c) *Types of Ticket*

There are several types of 'saver' ticket available on French railways, which enable savings of up to fifty per cent off the normal fare:

1. Frances Vacances pass. This provides unlimited first and second class rail travel throughout France on any four days during a period of fifteen days or on any nine days during a period of one month.

2. Holiday Return ('Sejour') ticket. Twenty-five per cent reduction on a return or circular journey of at least 1,000km.

3. Rail Europ Family (REF) card. This costs £5. With it one member of a family group pays full fare whilst all the others qualify for a reduction of up to fifty per cent on rail travel and up to thirty per cent on channel crossings.

4. Rail Europ Senior (RES) card. This is available to those over sixty who are holders of a BR Senior Citizen Railcard. A RES card holder is entitled to up to a fifty per cent discount on rail travel and up to a thirty per cent reduction on Channel crossings.

5. For those under twenty-six Inter-rail cards and 'Carte Jeune' are available. For the over twenty-sixes a more expensive European Inter-rail card can now be purchased. This is still good value for those intending to travel extensively by train before or after the RLS Trail.

Further details can be obtained from major BR travel centres and from most railway stations in France. Note also that there is an English language train information service in Paris. This can be dialled on 45.82.08.41.

One cautionary note. Access to railway station platforms is free in France, but tickets must be validated by date stamping before boarding the train. This simple task is performed using the orange coloured machines (*composteurs*) which are located on the concourse of nearly all French railway stations. Failure to do so can result in a fine.

Coach

There is not an extensive network of long distance coaches in France comparable to that in the UK. However, Eurolines operate a number of services to France from Victoria coach station in London. Long distance coach is probably the cheapest way of travelling to and from the RLS Trail. Bookings can be made and further information obtained from principal National Express offices throughout Britain.

The main services of interest are as follows:

JAN 93
£82
RETURN

1. London to Lyon. A daily service (except Sunday) operates during the main summer season. Approximate journey time: 15 hours.
Le Puy for the start of the Trial can be reached by train from Lyon (see under 'Train').

JAN 93
£107
RETURN

2. Avignon to London. A service operates five days a week during the main summer season. Approximate journey time: 19 hours. A bus can be taken from St Jean du Gard at the end of the RLS Trail to Alès from where a main line train can be taken to Avignon to catch the coach home.

3. London to Paris. An inexpensive coach service operates between the two capitals several times a day. This could be used to reach Paris from where a train could then be taken to Le Puy for the start of the holiday.

These coach services are direct and luggage deposited at the start of the journey need not be retrieved until the destination has been reached, with the exception of carrying one's luggage through

British customs on returning to the UK. Several stops are made en route except on the London-Paris run which is non-stop.

Private Transport

There are two disadvantages of driving a car to the Velay/Cévennes when planning to walk the RLS Trail in its entirety. Firstly the car will have to be parked somewhere for the duration of the holiday. Sometimes a car can be left in a hotel car park provided that a night or two is spent in the hotel at the start and finish of the trip. The second disadvantage is that with a linear route such as the RLS Trail, public transport will have to be used anyway at the end of the walk to get back to the car left at the start (or alternatively to get to the start of the trail if the car is left at St Jean du Gard). For these reasons the use of private transport is not recommended.

It is useful to understand the road classification in France. Motorways (*autoroutes* or 'A' roads) are toll roads. Although fast, it is fairly expensive to travel across the country by autoroute. The speed limit on *autoroutes* is 130km/hr (81mph). 'N' or 'R.N.' (*routes nationales*) are roughly equivalent to British 'A' roads. 'D' or *département* roads are equivalent to British 'B' or 'C' roads. The speed limit on dual carriageways is 110km/hr (68mph) and 90km/hr (57mph) on single carriageways. In built-up areas the speed limit is 50km/hr (31mph) unless otherwise indicated. Radar speed traps operate in France and French police can inflict on-the-spot fines. Both front and rear seat belts are compulsory as in Britain. It is advisable to carry a red warning triangle in case of accident or puncture and to obtain a Green Card level of insurance.

HOTEL ACCOMODATION

Hotels in France are star graded on a system very similar to that in use in Britain. The basic hotel is the one star establishment and this is usually reasonably priced, clean and comfortable. Most of the hotels in the area covered by this guidebook carry a one or two star grading. Hotels are generally much cheaper in France than in Britain; expect to pay between 90 to 180FF per night for a room for two. One pays for the room ie. there is seldom a reduction if only one person occupies the room.

Many walkers on the RLS Trail will wish to use hotel accommodation for most or all of their overnight stops. The 'Facilities-Accommodation' sections of each chapter summarise the options available at the end of each day stage. In most cases hotel accommodation should be found at the end of each day, but the following notes should be considered carefully.

1. The majority of French take their holidays between mid-July and mid-August (Bastille Day to the Feast of the Assumption). There is a greater possibility of finding hotels full during this period than during any other time of the year. If possible try to avoid this high season if planning to use hotel accommodation exclusively. However, the Cévennes and Velay are not so popular with holidaymakers as certain other regions of France and even in the height of the summer season rooms can often be found.

2. Several hotels are closed throughout the winter months. Those which serve the ski resorts of the Cévennes have a second high season during the winter. The latter hotels are often closed 'between seasons', during early spring and late autumn.

3. Things change: new hotels are sometimes opened whilst others occasionally close. Try to glean the current situation on facilities ahead on the trail from other walkers, hoteliers, *gîte d'étape* wardens (and notice boards) and tourist offices. If difficulties are being experienced then try to phone ahead to book accommodation. Good spoken French will be necessary as few locals will understand sufficient English.

4. Sometimes hotels or restaurants have associated outbuildings or attics. These *dortoirs* provide basic, cheap accommodation for the night. Some villages, whilst not boasting a hotel, may have an *auberge* which is a simpler sort of establishment, often with rooms above a café or restaurant.

5. A list of hotels in the area will be found in the local *syndicat d'initiative* or *maison de tourisme*. The staff here will often book hotel rooms on your behalf.

6. Always read the 'Facilities-Accommodation' sections in this book for several days ahead in order to identify any areas where there could be difficulties.

7. It may be necessary to use the occasional *gîte d'étape* (q.v.) This

will be no real hardship and will provide greater opportunities for meeting other walkers on the RLS Trail and on the *Grande Randonnée* (q.v.) routes in the area.

8. Finally, if the situation seems hopeless, do not panic - something will turn up - it always does! A local bar will have a phone which can be used to book hotel accommodation 'off route' and to summon a taxi (cheaper than in Britain) to travel to the night's accommodation.

GITES D'ETAPE

There are several thousand of these simple hostels found all over France, particularly along the *Grand Randonnée* trails (q.v.). They provide basic and cheap accommodation for the outdoor enthusiast, especially the walker. There are several of these establishments on or near to the RLS Trail (see Appendix One) although there are few on the northern section of the walk before the Cévennes proper is entered. They should not be confused with *gîtes ruraux* which are basically holiday homes.

Gîtes d'étape come in all shapes and sizes, from converted barns or stables to large houses or parts of hotels. Few are purpose-built. The wardens are often farming folk who use the gîte d'étape as an extra source of income. The typical *gîte d'étape* will accommodate between ten and thirty people in a unisex dormitory, usually on large mattresses. It will have a kitchen equipped with stoves and cooking utensils and there will also be a dining area. There are usually hot showers as well as washbasins and toilets. The warden often does not reside in the *gîte d'étape* but may live in an adjacent house or farm. Meals are often provided by the guardian and these generally represent good value for money.

Most of the *gîtes d'étape* on or near the RLS Trail belong to one of two organisations: Chamina (Association pour le Dévelopment de la Randonnée Pédestre dans le Massif Central) whose logo is a green walking man equipped with cloak and walking stick; and ATR (Association de Tourisme de Randonnée Languedoc-Roussillon). However, it is not necessary to be a member of any organisation in order to spend the night at a *gîte d'étape*. No discount is offered to members of any clubs or associations. *Gîtes d'étape* provide inexpensive accommodation, usually with a fixed price for all the establishments belonging to a particular organisation. For example, all Chamina *gîtes d'étape* charged 30FF for overnight accommodation during 1990.

Gîtes d'étape are primarily intended as overnight accommodation for walkers hiking the various trails, so one is not normally encouraged to spend more than a few nights at any one *gîte*. They do, however, make ideal bases to sit out a spell of bad weather in the company of other like-minded people. Sometimes a small fee is payable for use of the *gîte* during the daytime. *Gîtes d'étape* can on occasions become very crowded, although this is less common in the Velay, Ardèche and Cévennes than it is in the more popular walking and climbing areas, such as the Alps. The warden will usually seek to accommodate everyone however full the *gîte*, but sometimes late arrivals may have to go elsewhere. But if there is no other accommodation available in the vicinity it is most unlikely that entry would be refused however full the *gîte*, although it may then be necessary to sleep on a mattress on the floor.

It is possible to book ahead by telephone, but good spoken French is necessary for this, as few guardians speak English. Overcrowded *gîtes d'étape* are most frequently encountered between mid-July and mid-August. Arriving early at a *gîte d'étape* is the best way of reserving a bed for the night. Remember also that dinner, if provided, is usually served from 7-8pm at most *gîtes d'étape* and therefore a late arrival will go hungry if not carrying his or her own food provisions.

CAMPING

There are two ways in which camping can be used to provide a means of accommodation along the RLS Trail. Firstly, purists may wish to camp wild along the trail, 'à la Stevenson'. This area of France is not ideal today for wild camping (*camping sauvage*), permission being required unless the camp is made high up in the mountains well away from habitation and roads. An uncontaminated water source will have to be located unless sufficient water is carried from a town or village. The art of the backpacker is to leave no sign of an overnight camp. Leave no litter and take care not to pollute water sources. Particular care should be exercised with matches and stoves as forests fires are all too common during the hot, dry summers. Do not light open fires.

Alternatively, walkers on the RLS Trail can stop each night at official campsites, of which there are many along the way. By carrying a small lightweight tent all problems of accommodation will be solved at a stroke. Walkers who do not normally camp out may wish to consider this type of accommodation for the RLS Trail. As restaurants and cafés are fairly numerous along the route it is not necessary to carry stove, cooking utensils, cutlery or extra food. The weight of a small lightweight tent can be shared between two to three people, although each person will need to carry a sleeping bag and insulating mat. During the summer months the climate is generally warm and dry (although violent thunderstorms do occur) and camping in this region of France can be very pleasant.

It is usually necessary to provide passport details and complete a registration form when staying at a campsite in France. The facilities at the various campsites on or close to the trail vary considerably from spartan (merely a water tap) eg. *camping à la ferme*, to luxurious, with bars, restaurants, sports facilities, etc. Most, but not all, of the campsites along the route provide hot showers.

FACILITIES EN ROUTE

Details of the various facilities available en route are given under each 'day' of the walk in the guide section. These are divided under the sub-headings of 'Accommodation' (hotel, *gîte d'étape* and campsite information), 'Restaurants/Cafés/Bars', 'Shops' (meaning a shop where foodstuffs may be purchased), 'Tourist Office' (if available) and 'Public Transport' (bus and train information).

Certain 'mobile shops' (grocery and bakers' vans) operate in some of the areas through which the RLS Trail passes. These drive from village to village and are most important to the local inhabitants in depopulated areas which cannot support a normal shop. They can also be useful to the wayfarer provided he/she is in the right place at the right time. It is worth keeping an eye open for these mobile shops. Sometimes *gîte d'étape* guardians or hoteliers can tell you when the mobile shops are due to visit the village.

Remember that things always change, particularly in these depopulated regions of France: *gîtes d'étape* and hotels sometimes open whilst old ones occasionally close down; shops close and bus and train services change. Other wayfarers, particularly those who have come from your destination, are a good source of current information, as are *gîte d'étape* wardens, hoteliers and other locals. The author would like to be informed of any changes to the facilities along the trail so that these might be incorporated into future editions of this guidebook. Please write with full details % Cicerone Press.

It is important to ensure that sufficient water or other drinks are available when walking the trail, particularly during the hot summer months and when there are no cafés or shops encountered during the day's walk. Never rely on finding drinks along the trail, but always carry sufficient liquid to last for the day. Otherwise dehydration, heat exhaustion or worse could be the result.

Public transport is not in plentiful supply in the Velay, Gévaudan and Cévennes, but few real problems should be encountered. This is particularly so if intending to walk the entire trail, when public transport will only be required for the start and at the end of the walk. The two disused railway lines encountered on the RLS Trail, which were either in operation or under construction when Stevenson passed this way in 1878, would be extremely useful to the modern foot traveller if they were in operation today. There are two lines still in use, viz. the Cévenol Line from Paris to Nîmes passing through the region at Langogne, La Bastide-Puylaurant, Villefort and Alès; and the branch line from La Bastide-Puylaurant to Chasseradès and Mende.

EATING OUT

France is of course renowned for its cuisine and one of the delights of a walking holiday in the Cévennes is the opportunity to eat out at several different establishments. Most restaurants have a range of fixed-price menus as well as 'a la carte'. Fixed price menus in most restaurants in the Massif Central range from 50FF to approximately 160FF (approximately £5 to £16, 1991 prices). The average meal costs around 60-80FF. For this price there is usually a choice of hors d'oeuvre, a main course (usually a meat or fish dish) and sweet, fruit and/or cheese. Wine is generally extra but it is of course much cheaper than in Britain. The 160FF menu would probably be a five or six course affair. It is a good idea to finish the holiday with such a meal as a 'celebratory dinner'. In summary, eating out in restaurants in France is in general cheaper than in Britain and the choice of establishments is much greater. The smallest village will often have one or more restaurants and even in the most isolated and rural parts of the country one can expect food of high quality at reasonable cost.

There are a few differences between eating out in France compared with Britain that should be appreciated. Firstly, the menus for lunch and dinner are usually the same, ie. lunch is a large meal in France. Most walkers will prefer to eat their large meal of the day in the evening, but occasionally it might be appropriate to walk in the morning and evening and escape the heat of the day in a restaurant over a long, slow lunch. Note that if a snack is required at lunchtime then this can often cost nearly as much as a full meal. Dinner is not normally available until 7-7.30pm. Breakfasts are 'continental' consisting only of coffee or drinking chocolate with bread and jam (average cost 15-25FF in 1991). Lastly, one small point: the same knife and fork are generally used for most courses on the menu; do not expect to get a clean knife and fork with every course.

Many restaurants in France are hotel-restaurants, but almost always meals are available to non-residents. Quite often a restaurant will double as a café or bar and will serve drinks and snacks to customers not requiring a meal.

Several *gîtes d'étape* on or near the trail also provide meals. Food in *gîtes d'étape* is generally of the same quality and price as in a restaurant. The evening meal at the *gîte d'étape* at Goudet can be particularly recommended.

Vegetarians will find life generally a little more difficult in France than in Britain. However, vegetarian meals are becoming more widespread in France, particularly in the cities and fashionable towns. If there is no vegetarian dish on the menu then give your requirements to the waiter; a vegetarian alternative will nearly always be provided on request.

EQUIPMENT

The amount and type of equipment taken depends very much on whether the walker intends to use hotel and *gîte d'étape* accommodation or to camp out most or every night, 'a la Stevenson'. The most important consideration, always, is to ensure that the pack is as light as possible; do not take unnecessary items - remember RLS's egg whisk! Nothing spoils a walking holiday more than having to endure the excessive weight of an overloaded rucksack; remember that, unlike Stevenson, you will probably have no donkey to carry your pack.

Parts of the trail along tracks and country lanes could be safely walked in a good pair of training shoes, particularly during the drier summer months. However, for the whole trail, and especially in the more rugged terrain of the Cévennes mountains, a pair of lightweight boots is recommended, preferably well broken in. Heavyweight mountain boots should not be necessary. Some form of lightweight shoe is also desirable for relaxing in the evenings and for rest days and general sight-seeing. The wearing of boots inside *gîtes d'étape* is not allowed and is discouraged in most hotels.

During the summer months this region of France usually experiences fairly high temperatures during the daytime, but, at an average elevation of around 1,000m (3,278ft), it can become decidedly chilly once the sun has gone down. Therefore for much of the time shorts and a tee-shirt will be the most comfortable attire, but warm clothing should also be carried to allow for possible deterioration in the weather and for evening use. It is useful to pack a pair of lightweight walking trousers which can be worn on the occasional cold day or to protect sensitive skin against sunburn. Such trousers can also be worn whilst relaxing in the evenings. Obviously, if walking during the spring or autumn then more warm clothing will be required; Stevenson experienced some cold conditions on the first part of his journey in late September. A waterproof and windproof jacket is essential at any time of the year and many people will wish to carry waterproof trousers.

The glare and heat from a southern summer sun can be intense, particularly during July and August. The use of a sunhat, high

The chapel of St Michel de l'Aiguille perched on the summit of the Rocher St Michel in Le Puy. (Day 1)

The ruins of the Château de Beaufort on the hill above the Loire at Goudet.
RLS made a sketch of this scene. (Day 2)

Above the infant River Loire on the GR3. (Day 2)

factor suncream, lip salve and sunglasses will all help to avoid over-exposure to the sun. To ensure that fluid is readily available during the day, at least a one-litre bottle should be carried per person. Mineral water is often sold in screw-cap plastic bottles in France and these can provide useful additional water carriers.

The rucksack, the size of which will depend on whether or not camping equipment is to be carried, is probably the most important item of gear. It is vital to inspect the sack thoroughly for wear before leaving for France. Try to ensure that the carrying mechanism is not likely to break whilst on holiday. A 'dustbin liner' for the rucksack and a supply of plastic bags should keep the contents dry in heavy rain. Equipment is best packed in different coloured 'stuff sacks' to enable easy identification and access to various items. Perishable food is best kept in a disposable plastic bag to prevent the accidental soiling of the inside of the rucksack.

The backpacker will need to carry additional equipment, a small lightweight tent being the main requirement. A closed-cell type of insulating mat is advisable to cut down body heat loss from the ground. A sleeping bag is essential, although a lightweight bag is probably satisfactory during the summer months (note, however, that the temperature can drop dramatically at night even during July and August). Those walkers intending to make use of several *gîtes d'étape* may also wish to consider taking a lightweight sleeping bag, as blankets are not always available.

The camper who also intends to cook his or her own food will need some form of camping stove. The most convenient type to use in France during the summer months is the camping gas stove. Spare gas canisters are readily available in France at campsites and village shops. Methylated spirits (*acool à brûler*) and lead-free petrol can also be purchased in France. If travelling by air it is important to remember that none of these fuels can be carried on board an aircraft; they will have to be purchased on arrival in France. A small cooking set and lightweight cutlery will also be required. Don't forget a box of matches or lighter.

There are several miscellaneous items to consider. It is wise to include a small first-aid kit to treat any minor cuts and bruises, headaches or stomach upsets. Insect repellent may also be found useful. A small torch may come in handy and a mini French/

English dictionary or phrasebook may help with communication. A Swiss army knife or similar will provide a sharp blade for cutting (eg. bread, salami), a pair of scissors, a can opener and a corkscrew.

Modern day travellers are advised to go without a donkey! It is, in fact, possible to hire donkeys from certain establishments in the Cévennes for the purpose of trekking and some parties of walkers may well be seen leading (or not, as the case may be!) these pack animals. Having observed the antics of two or three such donkeys and their exasperated masters, the author has concluded that the unwillingness and stubbornness of Modestine was not unique to that individual animal! If you must take a donkey then these can be hired from M. André du Lac, Rando-Fugères, Fugères, Saint-Martin, 43150 Le Monastier-sur-Gazeille. Tel: (010 33) 71.03.80.07 or 71.03.82.30.

Last but not least, many walkers will wish to take along a copy of Stevenson's *Travels with a Donkey in the Cévennes* (see Bibliography) for to walk this trail is to make a literary and historical pilgrimage. However, the wayfarer is advised to take a guidebook (preferably this one!) and the relevant maps as well, for Stevenson left no doubt that he was a writer, not a geographer (as he was at pains to explain to Father Apollinaris at the Monastery of Our Lady of the Snows). *Travels with a Donkey* is in no sense a guidebook to the trail and it is sometimes a matter of conjecture as to the exact route taken by RLS. However, to refer whilst on the walk to Stevenson's accounts of the various places along the way and the people he encountered will add much to the pleasure of this journey.

GRANDES RANDONNEES

France has a very extensive network of official long distance paths called *Grandes Randonnées* (literally 'big walks') commonly abbreviated to GR. Each GR route has been designated a number eg. GR7, GR65, etc. The principal long distance trails usually carry a low number eg. GR4, GR6, whereas shorter, circular routes, variations or links have two or three digit numbers. Trails in the vicinity of a 'one digit' GR route all carry the same first number. For example the GR4 has the associated GR43, 44 and 412; the GR6 has the associated GR60 and 65, and so on. This system has analogies with the road numbering system in Britain: M6, M62, etc. Note that GR routes which are circular are generally referred to as 'tours', eg. Tour des Cévennes. There are at present some 25,000 miles (40,250 kilometres) of GR trail throughout France and the network is still expanding.

The RLS Trail is rather an oddity in that it has not as yet been incorporated into the GR network of long distance paths in France. To distinguish it from a GR route, the RLS Trail is waymarked with blue paint stripes, whereas all GR trails are traced with red and white markings (see Waymarking and Navigation). Although the RLS Trail is not itself a GR route, it frequently makes use of existing GR trails on its journey south to St Jean du Gard. Many French and English ramblers hope that with improved waymarking and better facilities en route, the RLS Trail will eventually be designated as a GR route.

The RLS Trail passes through splendid walking country in the Velay, Gévaudan and Cévennes and it is therefore not surprising that these regions are criss-crossed with an extensive network of GR trails. Stevenson's route crosses or uses part of eleven GR trails in all, further details of which are given in Appendix Two. They can be used for further exploration of the surrounding countryside, as link routes to neighbouring towns and villages and finally as ideas for future holidays in the Massif Central. In addition to the long distance trails there are many shorter, regional footpaths referred to as *GR de Pays* and *Sentiers de PR' (Petite Randonnée)*. Information on all the walking routes in the Massif Central, together with accommodation details, will be found in the Chamina publication entitled *'Le Colporteur - La Randonnée France - Massif Central'*. The magazine, produced annually, is widely available in this region of France and copies will no doubt be seen in the *gîtes d'étape* along the RLS Trail.

Note added on going to press: In 1991 the Stevenson Trail was finally adopted by the GR authorities (Fédération Française de la Randonnée Pédestre, FFRP). Minor alterations to the route are envisaged to reduce further the amount of road walking, and the trail is eventually to be re-waymarked. The trail will not be designated a GR number, but there are plans to waymark either using the word "Stevenson" or a donkey's head symbol. These modifications are unlikely to be implemented for several years, but walkers should look for new signposts and alterations to the route described herein.

WAYMARKING AND NAVIGATION

The RLS Trail is waymarked along most, but not all of its length, by simple blue paint stripes. These occur on rocks, boulders, trees, posts, fences, telegraph poles, etc. The paint is mainly light blue in colour but occasionally a darker blue paint has been used. Some of the waymarks are very faded and in places a newer paint flash has been made to replace a very faded old one. Much of this paint waymarking was carried out by volunteers in preparation for the centenary celebrations in 1978. Here and there the trail is waymarked with blue and white wooden St Andrew's crosses. These were erected along the route by March 1978, but many are now missing, having either been taken as souvenirs or else destroyed by disgruntled landowners. The trail between Le Monastier and Langogne was waymarked by the Le Monastier scouts as early as 1966-8, with small metal signs showing the head of a donkey. Alas, only one of these signs remains today (at Courmarcès - see Day 2).

This was the waymarking situation by summer 1990. Although not perfect, the waymarks, coupled with the use of the relevant map and the route descriptions contained in this guidebook, should be adequate for following the trail. It is hoped that it will not be long before the route is re-waymarked along its entire length to replace those which have been removed or have faded or become hidden by undergrowth.

Two further points of detail. Firstly, a very important, albeit fairly obvious one. A blue painted cross, X, indicates that to proceed in that direction is to follow an incorrect route. Secondly, just occasionally the blue paint stripe of the RLS Trail is accompanied by a white paint stripe (in the same way as the red of the GR trail is accompanied by a white stripe). Why this has been done is unclear to the author, but they indicate the correct route in the same way as the single blue stripe (although rather confusingly blue/white does sometimes signify a short, local walk).

There are several other trail signs that will be seen while on the RLS Trail and these should be understood and not confused with those of the Stevenson route. Wherever the RLS Trail is co-incident with a *Grande Randonnée* (qv), it will be accompanied by the standard painted red and white waymarks of the GR routes. In the GR waymarking system various arrangements of red and white lines are used to signify different instructions. When two sets of red/white marks appear together this signifies that a change in direction is imminent. This instruction is sometimes indicated by the use of curved red and white markings pointing towards the new direction to be taken. The painted cross, usually of one red and one white line, signals that the route is not in that direction; go back to pick up the correct trail. Remember also that *all* GR trails are waymarked with red and white flashes. In areas where two GR routes meet or where a variant leaves the main route, care should be taken to follow the correct GR Trail.

Other waymarks will occasionally be seen. Local footpaths or *PR (Petites Randonnées)* are waymarked in a variety of colours - single yellow or green paint stripes are fairly common. Orange waymarks are for bridleways; they sometimes occur in the shape of a 'hoof print', signifying a horse or pony trail. Certain notices should be understood. *'Propriété Privée'* or *Defense d'entrer'* means that the area is private and entry forbidden. The signs *'Réserve du Chasse'* and *'Chasse Privée'* do not refer to walkers, but indicate that hunting rights are reserved for the owner of the land.

The blue waymarks of the RLS Trail (at least in their present state, summer 1990) cannot be used as the only means of navigation; they act only as a guide indicating that the correct route is being followed. Use must be made of the relevant maps, and the ability to use both map and compass would be a distinct advantage. The route is intricate in places (eg. Langogne to Luc) but it is hoped that all problems will be solved by making use of the detailed route description provided in this guidebook. Particular attention has been paid to the route description in areas where difficulties in following the route may be experienced.

Some problems may be experienced in reading the finer details of the 1:50,000 IGN maps. The appearance of small 'white roads' on these maps usually, but not always, indicates that they are metalled (surfaced); sometimes they are only unsurfaced dirt tracks. Also a few of the tracks indicated by single thin black lines on the maps have now been made up to surfaced lanes. Hence care is required in order to avoid navigational errors. Parts of the route which have been described as dirt track in this guide, may in later years be surfaced. Therefore some care in interpreting the descriptions will be required

MAPS

The recommended maps for use on the trail are the IGN Serie Orange maps at 1:50,000. Seven sheets cover the entire route:

Sheet 2836	Le Monastier-sur-Gazeille
Sheet 2736	Cayres
Sheet 2737	Langogne
Sheet 2738	Le Bleymard
Sheet 2739	Génolhac
Sheet 2639	Florac
Sheet 2740	St André-de-Valborgne

It is not absolutely necessary to purchase all seven maps. Sheet 2836 (Le Monastier-sur-Gazeille) covers only the first three miles (4.8km) of the journey from Le Monastier to Le Cluzel, and most walkers should be able to cover this section without difficulty by reference to the route in this guidebook and by following the blue RLS Trail waymarks. However, the sheet does include several attractive and interesting areas of the Velay and Haute Loire, including the Mont Mézenc and Gerbier de Jonc (source of the Loire) regions and walkers wishing to explore further are advised to purchase this map. Secondly, the sheet 2639 (Florac) covers little more than a mile (1.6 kilometres) of the route (through Florac itself) and it is certainly unnecessary to buy this map unless time is to be spent exploring the Tarn Gorges to the west (recommended), in which case this sheet is indispensible. The other five sheets are, however, essential. It is useful to mark the route of the RLS Trail onto the 1:50,000 maps using a highlighter pen, prior to making the journey.

An alternative to the 1:50,000 maps is to use the IGN Serie Verte maps at 1:100,000. Only two sheets are required:

No.50	St-Etienne/Le Puy (Le Monastier to Langogne)
No.59	Privas/Alès (Langogne to St Jean-du-Gard)

Although the route of the RLS Trail is overlaid in orange on these maps (and marked as *Trace Historique Stevenson*) they are far less useful than the 1:50,000 maps for following an intricate cross-country route. Some walkers, however, may find them adequate when combined with the route descriptions given in this guidebook. They are certainly ideal for the initial planning of the route at home.

Another useful map to consider is the special IGN map of the Parc National des Cévennes (No.354). This, at a scale of 1:100,000, indicates the park boundary and a number of tourist facilities together with certain other useful information. The part of the route from Luc (Day 6) to St Jean-du-Gard is covered by this map. It is particularly recommended for those intending to explore the national park further, either after the walk or on another occasion.

In addition to these detailed maps, it is often useful to carry a cheap and lightweight small-scale map of France (1:1,000,000 is sufficient) to ascertain one's position within the country and for use when planning sightseeing or other excursions, if time is available at the end of the holiday.

Finally, for those who wish to plan further walking tours along the excellent GR Trails in France, the IGN (Institut Géographique National, the French equivalent of the Ordnance Survey) publishes a small-scale map of France (1:1,000,000) entitled *'Sentiers de Grande Randonnée'* (Sheet No.903). This shows the entire network of GR trails throughout the country.

All of the above maps can be purchased from the specialist map shops listed in Appendix Four (Useful Addresses).

STEVENSON'S ROUTE BY CAR OR CYCLE

This guidebook is primarily intended for walkers wishing to follow Stevenson's journey through the Velay and Cévennes on foot. However, it is perfectly possible for those unwilling or unable to walk the route to follow a similar itinerary by car or even on a bicycle. Indeed, as many of the tracks and paths used by RLS have now been incorporated into the modern road system, such a method would enable the actual route followed by Stevenson to be followed more exactly in certain areas, for example from Le Pont de Montvert to Florac down the valley of the Tarn on the D998. All the principal towns and villages visited by RLS can be reached using the road network. Much of the driving or cycling would be on pleasant, little used 'D' roads. The IGN Serie Verte maps at 1:100,000 would be more than adequate. This book provides information on facilities and places of interest along the route and so will be of use to those using a car or cycle. Allow at least two or three days if travelling by car to allow time to search out the places visited by Stevenson. Cyclists would be able to use some of the tracks followed on the RLS Trail, but are certainly not advised to attempt the whole route by bicycle.

MODERN TREKS ALONG THE RLS TRAIL

The first person to follow the route taken by Stevenson in the Cévennes and write of his experiences was a certain Mr Skinner in 1926. However, he made use of a motor car. The first to walk with a donkey was a woman, Miss Elizabeth Singer, in 1948, when she was twenty-one years of age.

In more recent times there have been three notable journeys along the trail. The first was that of Mrs Betty Gladstone, an American woman, who walked from Le Monastier to St Jean du Gard in May 1963, accompanied by her twelve and eighteen year-old daughters and a donkey. She became almost a legend in the Cévennes returning several times until, in the autumn of 1965, she donated the granite plinth which was erected outside the post office in Le Monastier to mark the place where Stevenson began his journey. This commemorative plaque was unveiled at a small ceremony by the late Mrs Nancy Brackett, President of the RLS Club of Edinburgh and a cousin of Stevenson. Mrs Gladstone died in 1990.

Exactly ninety-nine years after Stevenson had started his journey with Modestine, at daybreak on September 22, 1977, another American woman, Carolyn Bennett Patterson, set out from Le Monastier to follow in Stevenson's footsteps. She too travelled with a donkey, also christened Modestine, but fourteen years old and somewhat larger than the original Modestine. Carolyn Patterson was one of the senior editors of *National Geographic* magazine and the story of her journey, on which she was accompanied by a photographer, Cotton Coulson, appeared in the magazine of October 1978 (Vol.154, No.4, pp535-561). She tried to follow Stevenson's itinerary as closely as possible, although some changes in the route had to be made as certain sections of RLS's route were by then along fairly busy, motorable roads on which she couldn't travel safely with a donkey. She stayed overnight at the same locations as Stevenson; where he had stayed overnight at an inn then so did she and when he had spent a night under the stars, she did as well. When RLS spent the morning writing up his journal before setting out, as at Langogne, then so did Carolyn Patterson. She too stayed at the Trappist Monastery of Our Lady of the Snows and like Stevenson attended Compline and Salve Regina after dinner. Mrs Patterson finished her journey, like RLS on October 3, twelve days after setting out from Le Monastier.

The year after Carolyn Patterson's walk, 1978, was the centenary year of Stevenson's trek. To mark the occasion a group of six writers and outdoor journalists assembled at Le Monastier to retrace Stevenson's journey. The group was under the leadership of Rob Hunter (Neillands), a journalist and well-known writer on walking in France. Much of the organisation of the centenary celebrations and liaison between France and Scotland was undertaken by the Scotswoman and *Club Cévenol* member, Pat Valette, who is married to the Frenchman Pierre Valette, and lives in the Cévennes. This centenary walk was not a complete success as the temperature was very high with blazing sunshine every day, which led to heat exhaustion for a couple of members and bad blisters for others. Moreover, they did not take a donkey, no doubt a wise decision, but had to carry heavy packs containing camping gear instead, which all added to the general discomfort.

After attending a reception hosted by the local people, the party set out early one September morning, one hundred years after Stevenson, to inaugurate the newly waymarked trail. They were welcomed by many locals and holidaymakers at various points along the route, who often came out in force to offer encouragement. A mere seven days later, after a last camp at St Etienne-Vallée-Française, the walkers arrived at the end of the trail at St Jean du Gard.

Since the centenary year many thousands of walkers, as well as cyclists and motorists, have followed in the footsteps of Stevenson in the Cévennes and quite a few have written of their experiences. It is hoped that this trail guide will add to the enjoyment of all those who follow this classic route.

THE CLUB CEVENOL

The *Club Cévenol*, founded in Florac in 1894 by a Protestant minister, Paul Arnal, is the oldest and most active of the associations devoted to the Cévennes mountains and their in-habitants. The interests of the club also extend to the neighbouring limestone plateau of the Causses. The members of this non-profit making organisation belong to a number of different groups which include both resident Cévenols and 'expatraites' living in Montpellier, Nîmes, Marseilles and Paris, as well as several non-natives interested in the Cévennes and its future. The club's head-quarters, for many years in Paris, is now in the Chamber of Commerce in Alès.

The objectives of *Club Cévenol* are threefold: to safeguard the natural and cultural heritage of the Cévennes and the Causses; to encourage the maintenance and creation of activities that will enable the inhabitants of the Cévennes and the Causses to stay in the land of their birth; and lastly, while upholding the tradition of courtesy and hospitality in the Cévennes and the Causses, to promote only those forms of tourism which will preserve the special character of the area.

The club's journal or review, *Causses et Cévennes* which has appeared for more than ninety-seven years, is published quarterly under the editorship of Pierre Valette. Some of the more recent numbers have dealt with the revival of silk production, the transhumance of sheep and cattle, peripheral industries and the future of the coal basin, beekeeping, forests and fires, the Cévenol maquis, the chestnut tree and its influence and not least the travels of R.L.Stevenson and others.

Club Cévenol has produced a number of memoirs of notable

figures in the history of the Cévennes, as well as a recording of Cévenol folk songs, sung in the ancient language of Occitan by Jean-Noel Pelen (1980). However, the club is not only active in the cultural sphere, but under its current president, Philippe Joutard, rector of the Academie de Besançon, it is making its views known on any planning development likely to affect the way of life of the region. This is done by means of its review, the work of its council and action committee and the public debates it organises periodically to discuss the impact of tourism on the land and local communities. It has successfully campaigned in recent years against the building of a reservoir in the region which would have flooded and destroyed an historic Protestant valley and well-known beauty spot.

The commemoration of the centenary of Stevenson's journey in 1978 was due entirely to the efforts of the *Club Cévenol*, particularly the work and inspiration of Pat Valette, a Scottish woman married to the editor of the *Club Cévenol* review, who has lived in the Cévennes for many years. The Club produced *Le Journal de Route de Robert Louis Stevenson* (a co-edition with Privat, Toulouse) in 1978 to mark the centenary. This was prepared from the original notebook used by RLS whilst in the Cévennes, which was discovered in a Californian library by an American relative of a *Club Cévenol* member. The English version of this book - *The Cévennes Journal* was published in the same year by Mainstream Publishing, Edinburgh (see Bibliography). *Club Cévenol* also organised several other events to coincide with the centenary, including the waymarking of parts of the RLS Trail and a special centenary walk of the route (see Modern Treks Along the RLS Trail). The first bilingual *Topo-Guide* to the trail also dates from this period. *In Stevenson's Footsteps - A Guide to his Journey (Sur Les Traces de Stevenson - Topoguide de l'Itinéraire)* was the work of the Stevenson Centenary Committee. (Note that another Topo guide was published in 1985 by the Fédération Francaise de la Randonnée Pédestre. This consisted of a single folded sheet having a sketch map of the route together with a very brief route description in French and English.)

The *Club Cévenol* has been involved in the preparation of this guidebook, providing useful local information and offering valuable advice to the author (see acknowledgements). A French version of this guidebook is to be produced by the club.

43

SNAKES

The European viper or adder is not uncommon in the Massif Central, and a bite, although unlikely to be fatal, would be exceedingly unpleasant and could have serious consequences in the more sparsely populated regions through which the trail traverses where help may not be quickly available. Fortunately they are fairly secretive animals, likely to detect a walker's presence by vibrations along the ground and take evasive action. Nevertheless, keep a good look out for vipers in order to avoid accidentally treading on one. It is a good idea to familiarise oneself with the markings of the European viper (dark green/black in colour with characteristic zig-zag stripes on the upper surface) in order to identify a specimen if seen. The chances are that the trail will be completed without catching sight of even one of these reptiles.

A bite from a viper can result in considerable bruising, discolouration and swelling of the surrounding area. If bitten it is necessary to rest, avoid a panic reaction, get medical help as soon as possible and in the meantime try to suck out the venom. It is possible to buy an aspiratory device for this purpose in pharmacies in France (for example the pharmacy in Le Monastier at the start on the walk keeps a supply of aspirators). This device consists of a syringe with variously sized and shaped attachments, which enable venom to be sucked from a wound. It is also possible to purchase a viper venom antidote (antiserum) without prescription in French pharmacies. The application of this requires a self-injection in muscle tissue near the site of injury, but it should only be used in emergencies when medical help cannot be obtained (see under 'Insurance').

LANGUAGE

The French, like the British, are not particularly keen on learning foreign languages. Many of the younger people can speak some English, but in general do not expect the level of fluency found in Holland and Germany. The Velay, Ardèche and Cévennes are sparsely populated regions where many of the villages and hamlets have a preponderance of elderly people, who are able to understand only French. It is a good idea to brush up on 'rusty' French before the holiday; even the most elementary grasp of the language will pay

44

dividends by enriching the experience of walking in France. However, no true adventurer will be discouraged by an inability to speak the local tongue, even if it will necessitate the occasional use of sign language!

PHOTOGRAPHY

Most walkers will wish to have a photographic record of their journey along the RLS Trail. The best type of camera to take is probably the 35mm SLR; a wide-angle lens (eg. 28 or 35mm) is particularly suitable, while a telephoto lens will be useful for capturing details of more distant features. All of this camera equipment is unfortunately very heavy, but a compromise would be to use a medium zoom lens (eg. 28-80mm) on an SLR body. This would obviate the need to change lenses continually - nevertheless zoom lenses are themselves heavier than prime lenses. Weight can be radically reduced by using a good quality 35mm compact camera equipped with a reasonably wide-angled lens, or alternatively a zoom lens. The quality can be almost as good as an SLR camera, but the compact camera is light and small, easily fitting into a pocket.

Both used and unused film should be protected from heat by placing it well inside the rucksack. It is advisable to take all exposed film home rather than posting it back to Britain to be processed. It could be lost in the post or damaged by X-ray equipment in the sorting offices.

MONEY; BANKS

The unit of currency is the French franc (approximately 10FF to £1 sterling). It is advisable to carry a fairly large supply of moderately low denomination notes (50, 100 and 200FF notes are particularly useful). Besides cash, Eurocheques, travellers' cheques and credit cards are all widely used in France. Eurocheques are particularly convenient, the only problem being that sometimes a minimum quantity will have to be exchanged (1400FF in 1990) which is a nuisance if money is required at the very end of the holiday. Alternatively, travellers' cheques may be carried. French franc travellers' cheques are the most useful as these can sometimes be used in restaurants, hotels, etc., as immediate payment. Access and Visa cards are accepted widely in France and are a useful form of payment for restaurant meals and rail tickets. However, do not expect all of the establishments along the RLS Trail to accept this form of payment.

There are banks in Le Puy, Costaros, Landos, Pradelles, Langogne, Le Pont de Montvert, Florac, St Germain-de-Calberte, St Etienne-Vallée-Française and St Jean-du-Gard. However, some of those in the smaller towns and villages are only open one or a few days per week and then only for a few hours. The banks in the larger towns (eg. Le Puy, Langogne, Florac, St Jean-du-Gard) operate normal banking hours, which in France are from around 9am until midday and from 2-3pm until 4-5pm, Monday to Friday. Most banks are closed all day Saturday. The larger post offices (PTT) will cash Eurocheques, but several of those passed en route are the equivalent of British 'sub-post offices' and do not have such facilities. It is advisable to carry sufficient currency from the outset to avoid a long and time-consuming detour to a bank later in the holiday.

INSURANCE

It is advisable to take out travel and medical insurance for the duration of the holiday. As most of the RLS Trail follows clear paths and tracks it is unlikely that full 'mountain insurance' will be required, although it is best to ensure that the policy covers for this type of walking holiday. Several companies offer suitable policies (see Appendix Four).

There are cetain reciprocal rights available for British subjects in France under the National Health Service arrangements within the EEC. Information concerning eligibility for medical cover under this scheme and the necessary E111 form can be obtained from local DHSS offices. It is, however, not advisable to rely solely on Form E111.

TELEPHONE TO BRITAIN

It is becoming increasingly difficult for the visitor to make a simple phone call in France, due to the widespread introduction by French

Telecom of the phonecard system. During the late 1980s many of the public phoneboxes in France were converted from payphones to those requiring a phonecard. It is particularly difficult in the larger towns and cities in France. In Paris it is now almost impossible to find a public cash payphone, the one exception being in the foyer of Gare Saint-Lazare (there is normally a long queue!). There are more coin-operated payphones available in the villages and small towns of the Velay and Cévennes, but whether most of these will eventually be converted to those requiring a phonecard, is a matter for conjecture. Phonecards (for 50 and 120 units) can be purchased from most post offices and certain other advertised outlets. The only alternative is to use a phone in a hotel, café or restaurant, but it is very likely that a call made in this way will be much more expensive than in a public phonebox. The old style *jeton* or token system no longer operates in France.

The procedure for placing a call to Britain is very simple. Lift the receiver and insert the appropriate coins or phonecard, after which a dialling tone will be heard. The French have had a digital exchange system for many years now. First dial 19 (the code for an international line) and pause until a second dialling tone is heard. Next dial 44 (the code for the UK). Pause again before dialling the STD code of the number required, but minus the initial zero. Lastly dial the number of the line required. For example, to phone a number in Birmingham (STD code 021) dial: 19, pause, 44, pause 21 123 4567.

PUBLIC HOLIDAYS IN FRANCE

There are more public holidays in France than in Britain. Fortunately between June and October there are only two to consider, viz. Bastille Day on July 14 and the Fête of the Assumption on August 15. On both of these days the public transport system is considerably affected and many shops are closed, although most cafés and restaurants stay open. It is well to bear these days in mind and to plan accordingly, particularly if it is necessary to travel by public transport on either of these days. In addition, do not forget the public holidays in Britain which are different from those in France, if planning to leave or enter the UK on those days. In the spring there are public holidays in France on May 1 (May-day), May 8 (1945

47

Armistice Day) and on Whit Monday. In the autumn there are bank holidays on November 1 (All Saints Day) and November 11 (1918 Armistice Day).

For most of the year French time is one hour ahead of the time in Britain ie. French summertime is one hour ahead of BST and French winter time one hour ahead of GMT. For a few weeks in late September and early October Britain and France are on the same time (liable to change).

NOTES ON USING THE GUIDEBOOK

Layout of Guide

The RLS Trail has been divided into eleven stages each of one day's duration. A day in Le Puy before starting the trail is also recommended as is a final sight-seeing day at the end of the walk. Each walking 'day' has been designed to terminate where some form of permanent overnight accommodation should be available, usually a hotel, but sometimes a *gîte d'étape*. In general the days are not over-long, although there is some variation in the length and severity of each section, necessitated by having to reach suitable accommodation each night. Other possibilities for accommodation along the route are also given and it must not be assumed that the daily itinerary described here has to be adhered to rigidly. There are several possibilities for decreasing the length of the various stages and lingering a while, or for walking farther each day if this is felt desirable. Obviously walkers carrying a lightweight tent will have much greater flexibility for varying the itinerary. There should be sufficient information in this guidebook, with regard to the various facilities available, to allow the daily mileage to be varied as desired.

Each 'Day' stage in the book has been sub-divided into five sections as follows:

i) *Table*

This provides distances and estimated walking times between the various places en route. Altitudes above sea level are also given as an indication of the amount of ascent/descent involved. Hence basic details of the day's itinerary can be seen at a glance.

ii) *Facilities*

Details of accommodation, cafés, restaurants, shops, tourist offices and public transport encountered along the route. Reference to the 'Facilities' sections should be made several 'days' ahead to pinpoint any areas where certain facilities may be a problem.

iii) *Things to See; Places to Visit*

The main items of interest on or near to the trail are all summarised here, enabling the day to be planned more effectively. Reference to this section before setting out each day should avoid the possibility of forgetting or missing an important monument, building or view. Details of various longer excursions with sight-seeing options on a rest day or 'day-off' are also given in certain areas.

iv) *Travels with a Donkey* ·

This section outlines the adventures of Stevenson and Modestine on each particular stage of the journey. The places visited by RLS, the people encountered as well as Stevenson's deeds and thoughts are summarised, so giving an overview of his journey. Part of the fascination of this walk is to compare one's own trip with that of Stevenson's journey and identify the sights and places that he visited. Reading this section in conjunction with the relevant pages of *Travels with a Donkey in the Cévennes* prior to walking each stage should help to remind the walker of the events on Stevenson's original excursion. The various Stevenson quotes given are taken mainly from *Travels with a Donkey* but occasionally from his original journey as published in *The Cévennes Journal* (See Bibliography). All Stevenson quotes appear in italics.

v) *Route*

The final section is a detailed route description of the trail. When used in conjunction with the relevant IGN map, the wayfarer should experience little difficulty in following the way. Special attention has been paid to those areas where route finding may be a problem or where the waymarking is particularly poor. Where alternative routes are possible, details of these are also given.

Distances and Altitudes

Distances and altitudes are given in miles and feet respectively, because most English-speaking people are familiar with this system, and also in kilometres and metres because this is how they appear on the maps. A very approximate conversion is the following:
1,000m is approximately 3,300ft.
2,000m is approximately 6,600ft.

Timings

Times as well as distances are given between the various stages. These times are those that it is considered that the 'average' rambler would maintain, but no allowance has been made for stopping to rest and/or admire the scenery or to have lunch, etc. This must be considered when estimating the time required for the day's activities. The actual time taken will obviously vary enormously from group to group and on the prevalent conditions, but it is nevertheless useful to have an indication of the time generally required to walk a section. It is a system widely used in Europe. Occasionally, while on a part of the trail that doubles as a GR route, signposts will be encountered that indicate the time required to walk to the next village or *gîte d'étape*.

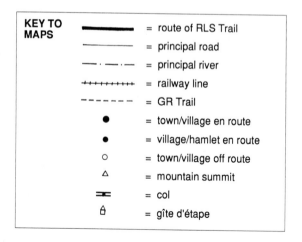

KEY TO MAPS		
▬▬▬▬	=	route of RLS Trail
────────	=	principal road
─ · ─ · ─	=	principal river
┼┼┼┼┼┼┼┼	=	railway line
─ ─ ─ ─ ─ ─	=	GR Trail
●	=	town/village en route
●	=	village/hamlet en route
○	=	town/village off route
△	=	mountain summit
⚏	=	col
⌂	=	gîte d'étape

THE GUIDE

SUMMARY TABLE

Stage		Distance		Est. Time
		miles	km	hr. min
1.	Le Puy en Velay	-	-	- -
2.	Le Monastier-sur-Gazeille to Costaros via Goudet	14.6	23.5	6. 00
3.	Costaros to Pradelles			
	via Le Bouchet St Nicolas & Landos	19.6	31.5	7. 55
	Optional excursion to Lac du Bouchet	(3.4)	(5.4)	(1. 10)
4.	Pradelles to Langogne	5.6	9.0	2. 15
5.	Langogne to Luc via Cheylard l'Evêque	16.4	26.4	7. 15
6.	Luc to Chasseradès via Notre Dame des Neiges	16.2	26.1	7. 05
7.	Chasseradès to Chalet du Mont Lozère			
	via Le Bleymard	11.2	18.0	5. 05
8.	Chalet du Mont Lozère to Le Pont de Montvert			
	via Le Col de Finiels	9.8	15.8	3. 50
9.	Le Pont de Montvert to Florac via Le Col de la Planette	14.8	23.8	6. 50
10.	Florac to Cassagnas via St. Julien d'Arpaon	11.4	18.3	5. 15
11.	Cassagnas to St Germain de Calberte	9.3	15.0	4. 45
12.	St Germain de Calberte to St Jean du Gard	15.2	24.5	7. 00
13.	St Jean du Gard / Alès / Nîmes	-	-	- -
	Totals	144.1	231.9	63. 15
		(+3.4)	(+5.4)	(+1. 10)

Le Puy.
The Rocher St Michel, topped with its 10th century Romanesque chapel,
is in the lower centre of the picture. (Day 1)

DAY 1:
LE PUY EN VELAY

FACILITIES

Accommodation
Le Puy possesses a large number of one, two and three star hotels.
There is a youth hostel in the upper town near to the cathedral. A
camp-site (three star) is situated about 1.2 miles (2 kilometres) out
of the centre of the town. It is signposted from near to the station.

Restaurants/Cafés/Bars
There is ample choice, from the simplest snack to haute cuisine.

Shops
As the principal town in the whole area, Le Puy has a wide variety
of shops and many banks. Large numbers of tourists are attracted
to the town, which specialises in lace-making by hand. Lace shops
abound. Although expensive, lace is unbreakable and light to carry
and is therefore suitable for walkers seeking presents for family and
friends, even at the start of the holiday.

Tourist Office
This is located in the Place du Breuil, adjacent to the theatre. Free
street maps of Le Puy are available from here as well as details of
hotel accommodation and information on local festivals, fêtes and
concerts.

Public Transport
Up-to-date train and bus information can be obtained from the
railway station (*gare*) and bus station (*gare routière*) respectively. Free
timetables are usually available.

Train
There are train services to St Etienne and Lyons (for the TGV to
Paris) and to Clermont Ferrand. Many trains stop at a number of
local stations.

Bus
There is an extensive network of bus services operating from Le
Puy, visiting most of the local towns and villages. However, the
major problem is that many of these operate only once or twice a day

and on only a couple of days a week.

The bus services of most interest to walkers of the RLS Trail are those between Le Puy and Le Monastier-sur-Gazeille, the start of the walk. There are four services which include Le Monastier on their itineraries.

1.   Le Puy-Coubon-Le Monastier-Issarlès.
2.   Le Puy-Coubon-Le Monastier-St Martin-de-Fugères-
         Alleyrac-Salettes.
3.   Le Puy-Le Monastier-Les Estables.
4.   Le Puy-Le Monastier-Le Béage.

These services are very limited, operating mainly on Wednesdays and Saturdays and usually on Mondays during school term time.

Le Monastier is only about 12.5 miles (20 kilometres) from Le Puy, and so a taxi would not be particularly expensive, especially if there are two or more in your party.

Another bus service of interest is that between Le Puy and Langogne. This is a daily service and stops at many of the towns and villages on the first stage of the RLS Trail, including Costaros, Landos and Pradelles. Finally there is a service on Wednesdays and Saturdays between Goudet and Le Puy, also stopping at St Martin-de-Fugères.

* * *

The great majority of walkers embarking on the RLS Trail will enter the region at Le Puy. Rather than make straight for the start of the trail at Le Monastier it would be much more sensible and rewarding to relax and unwind from the journey by exploring this picturesque and unique French town. A full day is recommended if time is available.

Le Puy-en-Velay, with a population of around 27,000, is the *Préfecture* of the *département* of the Haute-Loire. Situated on the River Loire, it is distinguished by a number of *puys* or pinnacles of rock, volcanic in origin, on which are perched some of the towns best known monuments. The highly photogenic tenth century Romanesque chapel of St Michel de L'Aiguille (St Michael of the Needle) is dramatically situated on the summit of the 80m high

Rocher St Michel. A series of steps leads to the top. The highest *puy* at 2,482 feet (757 metres) above sea level, is the Rocher Corneille on which stands the most famous landmark of Le Puy, the 112,000kg red statue of the Notre-Dame-de-France with the infant Jesus. This enormous statue, which is visible from most parts of the city, was made in 1860 from the metal of 213 melted-down cannons captured from the Russians at Sebastopol during the Crimean War. It stands 27 metres high and it is possible to climb up inside the hollow structure.

The twelfth century Romanesque cathedral stands half on the natural rock and half on pillars built into the hillside of Mont Anis. The influence of Moorish Spain and the East is seen in its Arabic and Byzantine features; the cathedral facade is particularly striking. Inside will be found one of the few surviving 'Black Madonnas of the Auvergne'. The abbey cloisters are worth a visit; the museum contains several fine frescoes including that of the Crucifixion.

The old centre is a maze of narrow streets dotted with lace-makers' workshops, well worth an hour or two's exploration. A small tourist 'train' (*Le Petit Train Touristique*) operates during July and August, taking visitors around the tiny streets of the town and up to the cathedral. Guided walks around the town and along the local GR and PR footpaths are also organised during the summer season; these of course, are given in French. Ask at the tourist office for details.

Le Puy is host to a number of festivals during the summer months. The procession through the streets by the brotherhood of the 'White Penitents' is quite spectacular. There is a pilgrimage to the town every August 15. Le Puy is one of the four traditional starting points in France for the pilgrimage to the shrine of St James at Santiago de Compostela in north-west Spain (the others being Paris, Vézelay and Arles). The modern long distance footpath, the GR65, follows a route of some 500 miles (805 kilometres) across France to enter Spain at Roncesvalles in the Pyrenees (see *The Way of St James - the GR65* by Hal Bishop, Cicerone Press). A further 400 miles (644 kilometres) or so along the northern edge of the Iberian peninsula leads to Santiago. The first steps on this long trail are out of Le Puy on the rue Jacques and the rue de Compostela.

In many respects Le Puy is a more fitting starting point for the walk south than Le Monastier. Those wishing to start their walk from here have an excellent route, the GR3, with which to reach Goudet (see Day 2). In so doing they would omit the first few miles of the RLS trail between Le Monastier and St Martin-de-Fugères, but would have an additional 18.6 miles (30 kilometres) from Le Puy to Goudet. The GR3, waymarked with standard red/white waymarks, takes about seven and a half hours to follow to Goudet. The route is from Le Puy via Espaly - St Marcel, La Roche, Dolaizon, Tallobre, Tarreyres, La Beaume, La Champ, Les Salles, Les Rozières and along the River Loire to join the RLS Trail into Goudet. An alternative would be to take the GR65 from Le Puy to La Roche and join the GR3 to Goudet from there. This route is marginally shorter.

LE MONASTIER SUR GAZEILLE TO COSTAROS
VIA GOUDET

Total distance: 14.6 miles (23.5km)
Total estimated time: 6hrs
Maps: IGN 1:50,000 sheet numbers 2836
                            (Le Monastier-sur-Gazeille) &
                            2736 (Cayres)

S = SECTIONAL A = ACCUMULATIVE	Height above sea level		Distance S		A		Est Time S	A
	ft	m	mls	km	mls	km	hr m	hr m
LE MONASTIER-SUR-GAZEILLE	3049	930						
ST VICTOR	3278	1000	1.6	2.5	1.6	2.5		
PETIT SALETTES	3344	1020	1.0	1.6	2.6	4.1		
LE CLUZEL	3082	940	0.6	1.0	3.2	5.1		
COURMARCES	3246	990	0.3	0.5	3.5	5.6	1.30	1.30
LE CROS	3114	950	1.2	1.9	4.7	7.5		
ST MARTIN-DE-FUGERES	3278	1000	1.2	2.0	5.9	9.5	1.00	2.30
GOUDET	2491	760	2.4	3.8	8.3	13.3	1.00	3.30
MONTAGNAC	3049	930	1.4	2.3	9.7	15.6		
USSEL	3377	1030	1.7	2.7	11.4	18.3	1.15	4.45
BARGETTES	3600	1098	2.0	3.2	13.4	21.5	0.50	5.35
COSTAROS	3511	1071	1.2	2.0	14.6	23.5	0.25	6.00

FACILITIES

Accommodation

There is a hotel-restaurant in Le Monastier, Le Moulin de Savin, down by the river on the RLS Trail. There is also a campsite here. If the hotel is full, then the wayfarer without a tent may experience some difficulties in Le Monastier. These can be avoided by either arranging to arrive in Le Monastier in the morning and then walking the first stage to Costaros without an overnight stop in Le Monastier, or if arriving in the afternoon, there should be time available to walk the 8.3 miles (13.3 kilometres) to Goudet where

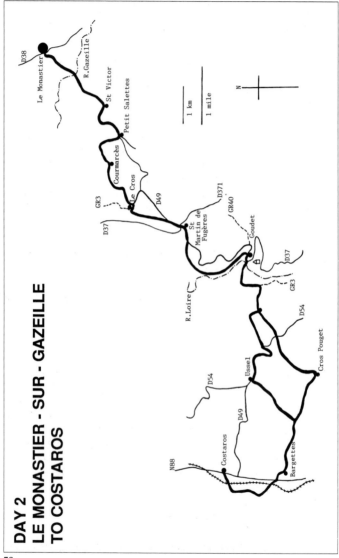

DAY 2
LE MONASTIER - SUR - GAZEILLE
TO COSTAROS

there is a *gîte d'étape*, hotel (Hôtel de la Loire, Tel:71.57.16.83) and campsite. There are several hotels in Costaros.

Restaurants/Cafés/Bars
There are several such establishments in both Le Monastier and Costaros. There is a restaurant and café (Café du Pont de la Loire) at Goudet, where the *gîte d'étape* also offers meals both to residents and non-residents (recommended).

Shops
There are several shops of all kinds (grocers, small supermarkets, fruit and vegetable shops, chemists, post offices etc.) in both Le Monastier and Costaros. There is a bank in Costaros. There is no shop in Goudet, but bread, cheese, etc. can usually be purchased from the guardian of the *gîte d'étape* and also from the campsite. A mobile bread van calls at Goudet (centre and campsite) first thing in the morning.

Tourist Office
There is a *syndicat d'initiative* in Le Monastier on the first floor of the *Mairie* (town hall). It is closed on Mondays.

Public Transport
For the bus service from Le Puy to Le Monastier see under Day 1 - Public Transport.

Other bus services of interest:
1. Le Puy-Goudet-Saint Martin-de Fugères
   Once or twice a day on Wednesdays and Saturdays only.
2. Le Puy-Costaros-Landos-Pradelles-Langogne-Mende. Several times each day. Hugon Autocars. The driver will also usually stop at Bargettes if requested. It is important to note that on these and most other local services, the buses will only stop when requested to do so, with the exception of the principal stops at the major towns. Bus stops or shelters are not often erected, and in these cases it is best to ask locals where to stand to await the arrival of a bus.

THINGS TO SEE; PLACES TO VISIT

Le Monastier
(i) *The Stevenson Memorial.* This rather grand title suggests rather

more than the somewhat crude mural found beneath the stairway in the *Mairie* (town hall). It consists of a thick rope attached to the wall, vaguely in the shape of the route taken by Stevenson, with adjacent place names, pictures and drawings. It was donated by the RLS Society of Edinburgh and erected in 1967.

(ii) *The Stevenson Plaque or Stèle.* This memorial commemorating RLS's journey is located under a tree outside the post office. It reads: *"D'ici Partit le 22 Septembre 1878 Robert Louis Stevenson pour son voyage à travers Les Cévennes avec un âne".*

(iii) The eleventh century Abbey Church of Saint Chaffre. It contains ecclesiastical treasure.

(iv) The thirteenth century château. Constructed of basalt rock, it has solid round towers topped with red-tiled roofs. There is a small Stevenson exhibition inside the building.

(v) The River Gazeille, a tributary of the Loire.

(vi) Views of the twin *sucs* of Mont Breysse, sketched by RLS during his stay in Le Monastier.

St Martin-De-Fugères
The church has an interesting seven-ribbed stone surround to the west door.

Goudet
The ruins of the château de Beaufort situated on a rock above the Loire, make a most impressive site in this deeply-cut valley. Stevenson made a sketch of the scene. The early morning is the best time for a photograph; the sun sets to the rear of the château producing a rather eerie silhouette.

Communal ovens. The hamlets of Montagnac and Cros Pouget both contain fine examples of roadside ovens, used until recent times by the whole community for baking bread. They are nowadays only used at the time of the village fête. Other examples of communal life can also be seen in these, now depopulated, villages of the Velay; for example, the bells on the roof of the village elder's house, used to summon the villagers together. One of the houses (rather hidden) in Cros Pouget has an interesting stone carving of the face of a woman. It is dated 1639 and is thought by locals to represent that of the

The 11th century Abbey Church of Saint Chaffre,
Le Monastier-sur-Gazeille.

queen, Marie de Médicis.

Arlempdes

About 1.5 miles (2.4 kilometres) south of Goudet. It is a village overlooking the Loire valley, with a castle perched on a rock above the river. It is worth a visit if at all possible.

TRAVELS WITH A DONKEY

"The best that we find in our travels is an honest friend. He is fortunate who finds many."

Stevenson *"spent about a month of fine days"* in Le Monastier before setting out on his travels. During this time he made several visits to Le Puy to purchase a huge sleeping sack which would *"— serve a double purpose - a bed by night, a portmanteau by day"*. He gathered together a large and odd assortment of kit including a revolver, jack-knife, spirit lamp, pan, lantern, candles, books and an egg-beater. His provisions consisted of a leg of cold mutton, a bottle of Beaujolais, chocolate cakes and tins of Bologna sausages. To carry all this he acquired, for *"65 francs and a glass of brandy"*, a donkey, *"a diminutive she-ass, not much bigger than a dog, the colour of a mouse, with a kindly eye and a determined under jaw"*. The animal was immediately christened 'Modestine'.

The pair set out at 9am on Sunday September 22, 1878, Stevenson having spent several hours since he rose just after 5am, attempting to load the donkey. The first day was not a success. The pace set by the donkey was frustratingly slow for Stevenson *"— it was something as much slower than a walk as a walk is slower than a run; it kept me hanging on each foot for an incredible length of time —"*. He soon took to beating the animal with a stick and in this way reached Goudet, where the rocky grandeur of the scene impressed him. He stopped to sketch the Loire and Château Beaufort and had lunch at the inn where he was shown a portrait of the landlord's nephew, *"Professor of Fencing and Champion of the two Americas"*, which is still in existence today.

Modestine was reluctant to climb the *"interminable hill"* out of Goudet (modern wayfarers may sympathise) and Stevenson became frustrated and exhausted with his efforts to coax the animal into a reasonable pace. To make matters worse, the enormous pack on the donkey's back would not remain upright and RLS was forced to carry several items of equipment himself. He thus was unable to control Modestine and was ridiculed by passers-by in his pathetic attempts to prevent the donkey from entering every house and courtyard in the village of Ussel. He soon decided to jettison several items of his kit, including the cold leg of mutton and the egg-whisk. But his troubles were by no means over as he headed west to Costaros which he described as *"—an ugly village on the highroad".*

ROUTE
Locate the plaque commemorating Stevenson's journey, under a tree in front of the post office in the High Street (D535) of Le Monastier. Walk south down the High Street for 50 yards and take the first small road on the right (signposted to the Hôtel/Restaurant Le Moulin de Savin). At once the walker is confronted with a plethora of painted waymarks, viz. a red/white GR waymark, a single yellow stripe (a local GR de Pays) and a single light blue stripe. It is the latter that is the waymark of the RLS Trail.

Continue down the road to pass a campsite and the above-mentioned restaurant. Cross the river by a bridge and continue on a well-defined track, climbing and following the blue and the yellow waymarks. The track heads to the south, then to the west for a while before swinging towards the east to meet the road (D500) just to the west of the village of St Victor (signpost on roadside). Turn right on the D500 and follow this for about half a mile (0.8 kilometres) to the village of Petit Salettes. At the junction of roads (the D500 and D49) take an unmarked, enclosed track heading north-north-west. This soon emerges into a field. Keep to the right edge of this field and leave it for another enclosed track. After one hundred yards or so, this turns to head east. At this point turn sharply to the left and follow an overgrown path (stinging nettles) through sparse woodland. This is somewhat tricky, but if one heads west a good track will soon be reached. Follow this and the blue waymark to the road at Courmarcès (change from IGN map 2836 to map 2736).

Soon take a waymarked track to the right of a barn. This reaches another metalled road in about 100 yards. Cross this and note the small RLS Trail sign (metal sign bearing the head of a donkey). This

Very dilapidated R.L.S. Trail signpost at Courmarcès

is one of the few remaining RLS signposts on the trail. Follow the sign along a clear red earthen track. After a while ignore another path leading off to the right, but instead descend to cross a small river (Rau du Cros) and climb to the village of Le Cros. After a few yards turn right at a concrete telegraph pole and descend and reascend on a marked track to a metalled road at a wooden telegraph pole. Turn right onto the road, but in about 100 yards turn left to follow a clear track for about 0.75 mile (1.2 kilometres) to the D49. Turn right and in 0.25 mile (0.4 kilometre) enter St Martin-de-Fugères. Walk through the village and take the D37 signposted to Goudet.

This road can be followed downhill to Goudet (the route taken by Stevenson — "— *I came down the hill to where Goudet stands in a green end of a valley* —") but a far superior route is as follows. After passing a cross on the left-hand side of the road, take a track heading down to the right (GR3). Follow the red/white waymarks. At one point the path approaches the road again over to the left, but ignore this and descend quite steeply through trees to reach the River Loire and turn sharply to the left (this change of direction is indicated by the double set of red/white waymarks). Follow the track, with river

The distant mountains of the Mont Mézenc range seen from near Bargettes on the RLS trail. (Day 2)

Above Cheylard l'Evêque. (Day 5). It was in this country between the hamlets of Fouzillac and Fouzillic, that Stevenson became hopelessly lost.

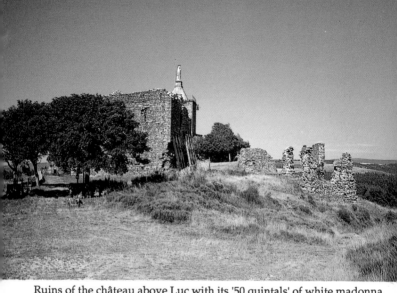

Ruins of the château above Luc with its '50 quintals' of white madonna.
(Day 5)

The view south from Les Alpiers. (Day 7). The plateau of
Mont Lozère is ahead in the distance.

to the right, all the way to Goudet.

Walk down through the village and turn right on the D49 (signposted to Ussel and Cayres) to cross the river by the road bridge. The ruins of Château Beaufort are clearly visible "—*opposite upon a rocky steep* —". The *gîte d'étape* is by the road bridge on the bank of the River Loire, opposite the telephone kiosk. The *gîte* is a converted barn; first enquire at the farmhouse.

An orange waymark (indicating a bridle-way) now joins the yellow, red/white (GR3 and GR40) and blue paint stripes. Follow only the light blue waymarks. Climb the D49 towards the west with the campsite down below on the bank of the River Loire to the right. After about 600 yards there is a path which ascends to the château. It is possible to explore the ruins of the château by taking this path, but it is not permitted to go further than the gatehouse (the ruins are in a state of disrepair and so can be quite dangerous). Leave the path that climbs to the château and instead take the track leading to a small bridge. Climb steeply on a path heading south. Eventually a tree decorated with numerous waymarks is reached. The GR3 continues to the south, but the RLS Trail, together with the GR40, turns right (west). Continue climbing the bank (good views down to the Loire and the château) to arrive at a large barn at a bend in a road. Turn right on this road to enter the village of Montagnac.

There are three alternative routes from Montagnac:

1. The "official" route (blue waymarks) via Ussel. Stevenson visited the village of Ussel where "—*saddle and all, the whole hypothec turned round and grovelled in the dust below the donkey's belly*".

2. A simplified version of 1. Continue on the road through Montagnac to "point 988" at a crossroads. Turn right here and descend by road to the river to join the route 1 to Ussel. Not recommended, but easy to follow.

3. Continue on the GR40, following the red/white waymarks to Cros Pouget and north-west to meet the D491, south-west of Ussel. This is the most interesting route; it avoids road walking and is easy to follow.

For the "official" trail, leave the GR40 red/white waymarks at Montagnac and follow the blue waymarks along a clear track. This at first heads towards the north, but soon turns to the west to meet the D54 near to a sharp bend in the road. Turn right on the road and

The gatehouse of the ruins of the Château de Beaufort above Goudet

follow it down to the river (La Bernarde). Cross the river and climb on the road, passing the junction with the D49 on the right and then that with the C9 to Fleurac (signpost to *"Camping à la Ferme"*, two kilometres). Continue into Ussel and leave the village on the D491 heading south-west. After about a mile the road reaches the GR40 coming up from Cros Pouget on the left. About fifty yards later, opposite the beginning of a small pine wood on the left of the road, take the track off to the right. This is waymarked with both red/white (GR40) and blue (RLS Trail). Soon the red roofs of the houses of Costaros are seen over to the right, but the first destination is the village of Bargettes. Much of the original track into Bargettes was newly surfaced in August 1989. Follow the waymarks through the houses to reach the main road, (N88, Le Puy to Pradelles.)

Costaros can be reached by turning right here, but a safer and more peaceful route is as follows. Cross the busy N88 with care and bear to the right on the track opposite. Climb up the embankment with a house on the left and pass a second house on the right immediately before a disused railway line (single track, overgrown). Follow the obvious track to reach a finger post for the GR40. Less than 0.5 mile (0.8 kilometre) from the main road take a track on the right leading to Costaros via the Croix-de-Montbasset.

COSTAROS TO PRADELLES VIA LE BOUCHET ST NICOLAS AND LANDOS. EXCURSION TO LAC DU BOUCHET

Total distance:	19.6 miles (31.5km)
Total estimated time:	7hrs 55min
Maps:	IGN 1:50,000 sheet numbers 2736 (Cayres) and 2737 (Langogne)

S = SECTIONAL A = ACCUMULATIVE	Height above sea level		Distance S		A		Est Time S	A
	ft	m	mls	km	mls	km	hr m	hr m
COSTAROS	3511	1071						
BARGETTES	3600	1098	1.2	2.0	1.2	2.0	0.25	0.25
PREYSSAC	3803	1160	1.7	2.8	2.9	4.8		
LE BOUCHET-ST-NICOLAS	3993	1218	1.6	2.5	4.5	7.3	1.20	1.45
AMARGIERS	3737	1140	3.7	6.0	8.2	13.3		
LANDOS	3606	1100	1.1	1.8	9.3	15.1	1.50	3.35
JAGONAS	3147	960	2.1	3.3	11.4	18.4		
ARQUEJOL	3301	1007	1.9	3.0	13.3	21.4	1.30	5.05
BEAUNE	3409	1040	2.1	3.3	15.4	24.7		
PRADELLES	3639	1110	4.2	6.8	19.6	31.5	2.50	7.55
Excursion to Lac du Bouchet:								
LE BOUCHET ST NICOLAS	3993	1218						
CROIX DE LA CHEVRE	4144	1264	1.1	1.8	1.1	1.8	0.25	0.25
LAC DU BOUCHET	3950	1205	0.6	0.9	1.7	2.7	0.10	0.35
LE BOUCHET-ST-NICOLAS	3993	1218	1.7	2.7	3.4	5.4	0.35	1.10

FACILITIES

Accommodation

The stage from Costaros to Pradelles is the longest on the entire route. This is necessary because of the lack of suitable accommodation between the two towns. It may be possible to find overnight accommodation in Landos, but a good choice of hotels (eg. Hôtel

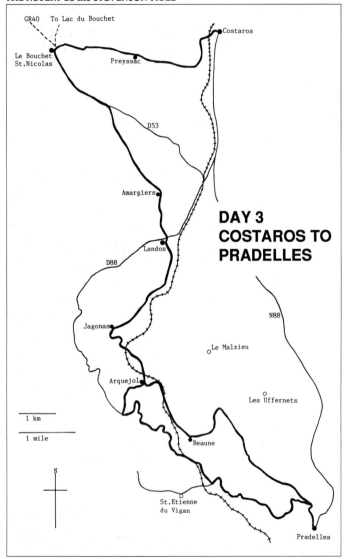

GR40   To Lac du Bouchet

Costaros

Le Bouchet
St.Nicolas

Preyssac

D53

Amargiers

**DAY 3
COSTAROS TO
PRADELLES**

Landos

D88

N88

Jagonas

Le Malzieu

Arquejol

Les Uffernets

1 km

1 mile

N

Beaune

St.Etienne
du Vigan

Pradelles

Bellevue, Hôtel Masclaux) is to be found in Pradelles, and so it is recommended that the walker makes this attractive and historic town his or her overnight destination. The walking is not particularly strenuous; after all Stevenson went farther than Pradelles in his first two days of travel, and he was delayed by the reluctance of Modestine.

Those wishing to make the excursion to the Lac du Bouchet (recommended) have an extra 3.4 miles (5.4 kilometres) to add to an already long day. However, it would be possible to break the journey at the Lac du Bouchet, where there is a hotel-restaurant by the lakeside.

Walkers carrying a tent are advised to divide Days 3 and 4 into two more equal parts by stopping the first day at the campsite about 1.25 miles (2 kilometres) to the north of Landos, alongside the D53, near to its junction with the D88. This campsite is marked on the IGN 1:50,000 map (nearest village Charbonnier) and can be reached by a short detour from the RLS Trail. The campsite has hot showers and provides meals if required. There is a small store (camping gas is sold). The second day can then be to Langogne, so catching up with the itinerary described in this book.

There are campsites close to Pradelles. The most convenient is reached by turning left at the junction of the D40 with the N88, when entering Pradelles on the RLS Trail. It is situated about 0.6 mile (1 kilometre) from this junction on the left-hand side of the road. The other campsite is a three star establishment with swimming pool. It is below the town on the N88, about 1 mile (1.6 kilometres) to the south of the centre of Pradelles. Both are marked on the IGN 1:50,000 map.

Restaurants/Cafés/Bars
There is a café and a restaurant in Le Bouchet-St-Nicolas and also at the Lac du Bouchet (excursion). There is a café and restaurant at Landos and a variety of restaurants and cafés in Pradelles. There is the Club Stevenson (a discotheque) about a mile (1.6 kilometres) north of Pradelles on the N88.

Shops
There is a well-stocked grocer's shop in Le Bouchet-St-Nicolas and a fairly large supermarket in Landos. Landos also has a baker's, butcher's and cold meat shop, as well as a bank. There is a good

selection of shops, supermarkets and a bank and post office in Pradelles.

Tourist Office
There is a *syndicat d'initiative* in Pradelles, in the Place de Foirail in the main street. This office will supply details of the history of the area and the annual *son et lumière*, as well as limited information on the RLS Trail and the connection with Stevenson.

Bus Services
1. Mende-Langogne-Pradelles-Landos-Costaros-Le Puy.
   Several times daily.
2. Le Chambon-St Haon-Le Bouchet St Nicolas-Cayres-Montagnac-Les Baraques-Le Puy.
   Once or twice a day on Wednesdays and Saturdays only (also on Mondays and Fridays during the school term).

THINGS TO SEE; PLACES TO VISIT

Wayside Crosses
A number of stone and metal wayside crosses will be seen along today's route and on the rest of the subsequent journey south. Some are many centuries old and have various types of ornamentation. These ancient wayside markers, protecting travellers from the evils of the road, are particularly common in the Velay, Auvergne and Cévennes. They often mark important crossroads.

Views of Mont Mézenc
The first stage of the walk provides opportunities for distant retrospective views of Mont Mézenc in the east. *"The view looking back was singularly wild and sad; the Mézenc and the peaks beyond St Julien stood out in trenchant gloom against a cold glitter in the east,"* Mont Mézenc at 5,747 feet (1,753 metres) the highest peak in this region of the Massif Central, can be climbed as a detour whilst walking the Tour of the Velay (see *Walks in Volcano Country* - Bibliography).

Preyssac
Note the interesting old contraption used for holding oxen while they were being shod. Oxen were often used to pull hay carts and the like. Several of these 'métiers à vache', now museum pieces, can still be seen in the villages and hamlets of the Auvergne. Note also

70

Stone carvings ('The Chase') at Le Bouchet-St-Nicolas

in this hamlet the hand pump for raising water from the well.

Le Bouchet-St-Nicolas
Note the interesting stone carvings dated 1810 on the old building opposite the general stores in the centre of the village. These depict a huntsman and animals. The latter could represent rabbits or hares, or perhaps even the Bête du Gévaudan. There are more carvings on the back and side of the building and in a few other places in the village.

Roman Road
A Roman road, La Voie Bollène, several miles in length, runs north-west/south-east through Le Bouchet-St-Nicolas. It can be followed as a track (the GR40) through the Lac du Bouchet Forest, all the way to Montbonnet in the north, a distance of some 7.5 miles (12 kilometres).

Croix de la Chèvre
The cross of the goat. It is decorated with a carved goat's head. Legend has it that a village once existed near the site of this cross. One night the inhabitants, with the exception of an old woman and

71

her goat, refused to give hospitality to a beggar. In revenge the beggar cursed the village and as a result it was engulfed by water, and all, save the woman and goat, were lost. It is said that at times the ruins of the village can be seen beneath the lake and that at night the church bell can be heard dolefully ringing.

Lac du Buchet

One of several volcanic lakes in the Velay. It is 92 feet (28 metres) deep, covers an area of approximately 43 hectares and has a diameter of about 0.5 mile (0.8 kilometre). It occupies the site of a crater created by an immense volcanic explosion. Other notable volcanic lakes in the area include that of St Front, north of Mont Mézenc and the Lac d'Issarlès, south-east of the village of the same name.

Landos

The village is built on the edge of an ancient volcanic crater.

The Railway

The Le Puy to Langogne disused railway line is encountered on several occasions on this section of the walk, principally at Bargettes and Costaros, Landos, Arquejol and Beaune. The line, built by the engineer Paul Séjourné, was opened in October 1912, long after Stevenson came this way. It was closed to passenger traffic in 1939, but was used for freight until April 1, 1988. Three kilometres of the line, between Le Puy and Brives-Charensac, are still in use. The rails remain in position and the station buildings (eg. the station at Landos) are still in existence. The line uses a number of bridges, the viaduct at Arquejol, seen from the RLS Trail, representing a particularly remarkable engineering achievement. The line joins the operational Paris to Nîmes main line just north of Langogne.

Rocher de la Fagette

A summit (4,147 feet; 1,265 metres) to the north-west of Pradelles. A superb view-point. The 'official' route passes close to this peak.

TRAVELS WITH A DONKEY

From Costaros Stevenson tried in vain to reach the Lac du Bouchet where he had intended to camp for the night. His map and/or his ability to read it were insufficient and he received little advice from surly passers-by. Moreover he was still having desperate problems with Modestine and her back-pack which fell to the ground for the second time on that first day. Thoroughly exhausted, less from walking than from thrashing Modestine, Stevenson arrived at Le Bouchet-St-Nicholas where he spent the night at an *auberge.*

RLS was well received at the inn where he found himself, much to his embarrassment, sharing a room with a married couple. The next morning the landlord presented him with a 'goad', a sharp pin at the end of a stick, which Stevenson found most effective in encouraging Modestine to follow the path. Thus equipped he continued to Pradelles, finding the road *"— dead solitary all the way —"*. RLS gave no indication of his route to Pradelles, but it was probably along what is now the D53 and N88.

"Pradelles stands on a hillside, high above the Allier, surrounded by rich meadows. —It was a cheerless prospect, but one stimulating to a traveller." RLS was now skirting the western rim of old Vivarais, leaving the Velay to enter Gévaudan, home a century earlier of the fabulous Bête du Gévaudan, a huge wolf or even werewolf, who reputedly *"ate women and children and shepherdesses celebrated for their beauty".* Wolves still roamed this remote, desolate country in the late nineteenth century and this was no doubt the main reason for including the revolver in his saddle-pack. The modern traveller need have no such worries and is advised to leave any fire-arms at home!

ROUTE

Return to the GR40 to the north-west of Bargettes. Take the track heading west that passes between the hills of La Gardine to the south and Le Péchay to the north. The route reaches a T-junction of tracks. Turn left and head towards the buildings of Preyssac seen ahead. A few hundred yards after Preyssac leave the main track on a small path to the left (follow the waymarks carefully). The path soon joins another track which climbs a little with a wood on the left. After a while Le Bouchet-St-Nicolas comes into view and the main track bears to the left. Leave this and follow a grassy track with fence on the right and low wall on the left aiming for the village clearly seen ahead (prominent church visible). Where the track comes to an abrupt end keep to the right-hand side of the field on the left, maintaining direction for the village. After four fields the route meets a gravel track which leads to a road (D31) by a stone cross and the sign for the village. Turn left to enter Le Bouchet-St-Nicolas.

If time is available for a visit to the volcanic Lac du Bouchet then take the minor road heading north to the Croix de la Chèvre. From here take the road and later the track descending to the lakeside. Refreshments may be had at the hotel-restaurant on the far bank of the lake, reached by the pleasant lakeside path. For a circular walk back to Le Bouchet-St-Nicolas, the GR40 'variante' can be followed from behind the restaurant to the north-west to reach "point 1243" on the D33 road. Here turn left and after about 0.25 mile (0.4 kilometre), at the Roman Road (Voie Romaine) turn left to follow the GR40 back into Le Bouchet-St-Nicolas.

In Le Bouchet-St-Nicolas leave the GR40 for the last time and turn left off the D31 to take the D53 heading south-east. Ignore an unmarked track on the right about 1 mile (1.6 kilometre) after Le Bouchet, but after another 0.5 mile (0.8 kilometre) take the track on the right, opposite a small overgrown pool on the left-hand side of the road. Another indicator of the correct track is the presence of a low concrete plinth labelled "2". A blue marker can also be found on a nearby rock. This track is the old road to Amargiers. Follow it all the way to the hamlet, where you bear to the right of the cross and water trough to take the road south. This becomes poorly metalled and leads to the centre of Landos.

At the crossroads in Landos bear slightly to the right to take a poorly surfaced road to the left of a small store. In about 0.25 mile (0.4 kilometre) take a fork off to the right on a grassy track. This leads in less than 0.5 mile (0.8 kilometre) to a cross-tracks at a stone cross near to the disused railway line. Here turn right on a track which soon becomes a narrow path with a fence on right. This widens into a grassy track which leads to a T-junction of tracks where you turn left and in 30 yards turn sharp right on the upper of two tracks. In a further 100 yards when the track forks, take the left-hand (minor) fork (railway line below to the left). Walk along this track on an embankment with a hedgerow on the right. At a T-junction turn right and continue along this track to the hamlet of Jagonas. The distant hills are those of the Cévennes where the RLS Trail is heading.

Immediately before the first building of Jagonas, turn left. In about 75 yards leave this surfaced track on a grassy path between low stone walls. In a further 150 yards leave this to descend to the right to a narrow, metalled lane, where you turn left (change from IGN map 2736 to map 2737). Descend to cross a stream (Vallon de Barges) and reascend on the now roughly-surfaced lane, ignoring a track ahead where the lane bends sharp left. Continue to cross the railway line *(Voie ferrée)* and follow the red, volcanic earth track to a metalled road. Turn right and descend towards the village of Arquejol.

Pass under the railway bridge and continue towards the buildings ahead. Where the road bends to the right (farm buildings on right-hand side) a decision must be made. There are two routes from here to Pradelles. The "official" route, waymarked with blue stripes, follows the line of the old railway track towards Beaune and then climbs to the north before resuming a south-easterly direction, along woodland tracks towards Pradelles. There is the minimum of road walking. The second route descends south to the Arquejol river to take the little-used D40 to Pradelles. It is easier to follow than the other trail, but involves quite a long section of road walking. This is the route marked on the 1:100,000 IGN map No.50.

1. *Official Route*

Where the road turns sharply to the right in Arquejol, take the grit track on the left. This descends into the valley soon revealing the spectacular eleven arched, redundant viaduct which carried the railway high above the river. Although the river is fairly small, there is quite a deep gorge at this point, and it was a considerable feat of engineering to span this valley. Cross the river by a small stone bridge and gently ascend on the grassy track, with good views back to Arquejol on top of the hill. On reaching an open area ignore the enclosed track bearing slightly to the right, but instead bear a little towards the left to pick up another grassy track which climbs very gently aiming for the railway seen ahead on the left. Pass under a railway bridge and follow the dirt track around to the right. Remain on this track, which follows the course of the railway seen down to the right, gently climbing to the village of Beaune with excellent views of the surrounding wooded hillsides.

Turn left at the road, climbing through the village, passing a stone cross on the right and continue on the poorly surfaced D284. This lane climbs first to the east, then the north and finally turns towards the north-east. When it does this, nearly a mile after Beaune, take a track off to the right. There are fine views over to the distant Naussac Reservoir, near Langogne. Pass under high tension cables and at a T-junction by a wooden pole carrying electricity cables, turn right onto another track (note: a single yellow paint stripe waymark joins the route at this point; part of the "Circuit Pédestre du Mazonric, PR125"). Ignore a track on the right, continue ahead descending slightly to a wet area, and about 100 yards after the track bends to the right, where the track surface changes to red volcanic ash, turn left uphill on a grassy track. Meet and turn left on a track heading uphill to the left of a small pinewood and turn right at a sandy track met at a bend. Enter woodland and take the right fork at a Y-junction. Emerge at a small clearing and here turn right, descending through the trees on a fairly narrow, somewhat overgrown path. Eventually Pradelles will be seen through the trees to the right. This path descends to the D40 road at a bend ("point 1142" on the map). Turn left to follow the D40 to a T-junction with the N88 at a stone cross. Turn left for the campsite, but right to enter Pradelles.

2. *D40 Route*

Keep to the road in Arquejol where it bends sharply to the right and descends to more houses. Climb on the road ignoring the road off to the right (signposted Landos) until about 400 yards beyond a stone cross on the left, and where the road curves to the right, take a red gravel path off to the left. Where this bends at right angles to the left, take the grassy track ahead to the D40 road, where you turn left. Descend to cross the river by a road bridge and remain on the D40 all the way to Pradelles, ignoring the D401 turn-off near St Etienne-du-Vigan. It follows the same general direction as the old railway which it crosses at one point. The route is scenic and easy to follow and there is little traffic along the road, even in the main summer holiday season. The "official" route joins the D40 from the left, just before Pradelles.

It may also be possible to follow the disused railway line for part of the way between Landos and Pradelles. However, it is very overgrown, difficult of access in some areas and probably dangerous in places. The author tried the short section between the D284 and where the line crosses the D40 (about one third of a mile). This was unpleasant; the option was either to walk on inconveniently spaced sleepers or at the side of the track which was overgrown (danger from snakes?). Not recommended.

Yet another route would be to follow the minor "white" roads from Landos to La Mouteyre, Les Uffernets, La Fagette and Pradelles. There is unlikely to be any traffic on these lanes, except for the odd farm vehicle.

DAY 4:

PRADELLES TO LANGOGNE

Total distance: 5.6 miles (9.0km)
Total estimated time: 2hrs 15min
Map: IGN 1:50,000 sheet number 2737 (Langogne)

S = SECTIONAL A = ACCUMULATIVE	Height above sea level		Distance S		A		Est Time S	A
	ft	m	mls	km	mls	km	hr m	hr m
PRADELLES	3639	1110						
LES BORIES	3147	960	2.5	4.0	2.5	4.0	1.05	1.05
LE MASEL	3213	980	1.1	1.8	3.6	5.8		
LE MAS NEUF	3039	927	0.9	1.4	4.5	7.2		
LANGOGNE	3000	915	1.1	1.8	5.6	9.0	1.10	2.15

FACILITIES

Accommodation

There are several hotels in Langogne. The food and service at the Hôtel Bel Air (a Logis de France, tel: 66.69.01.08) can be recommended. The Hôtel Gaillard, tel: 66.69.10.55, is also very reasonable. Those returning to Langogne from Luc on the following day may wish to book two nights in a hotel in Langogne (see Day 5 - Accommodation).

Langogne has two campsites. For the nearest and least pretentious (one star) turn left just after passing under the railway on entering the town. Follow the road to the left, passing back under the railway and climbing a little to reach the campsite on the left, a little under 0.5 mile (0.8 kilometre). It is marked on the 1:50,000 IGN map. The other campsite is the Camping de Naussac (two star) near to the Reservoir on the other side of the town (follow the road signs). This is perhaps more suitable if a rest day is planned in Langogne.

Restaurant/Cafés/Bars

There are numerous restaurants and cafés in Langogne.

DAY 4
PRADELLES TO LANGOGNE

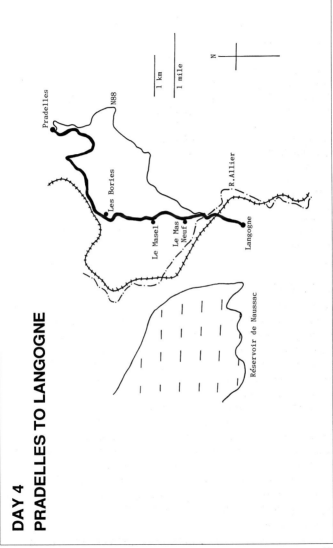

Shops

There are shops of all kinds in Langogne, as well as banks and a post office.

Tourist Office

There is a *syndicat d'initiative* in Langogne. It is situated a little way uphill from the old covered market.

Public Transport

Train Langogne is on the mainline railway between Paris and Nîmes. There are several trains a day to Clermont Ferrand, St Germain des Fossés and Paris (Gare de Lyon), and also to La Bastide, Alès, and Nîmes (for connections to Marseilles, Nice, Montpellier, Toulouse, Bordeaux and Avignon.)

Bus The service to Mende and to Pradelles, Landos, Costaros and Le Puy operates several times a day. A timetable can be obtained free from the *syndicat d'initiative.* The bus stops in the High Street outside the Café du Midi in the centre of town and also at the railway station (SNCF).

THINGS TO SEE; PLACES TO VISIT

Pradelles

There should be ample time available for exploring the medieval hill town of Pradelles before setting out on the short stage to Langogne. Pradelles has been declared a classified site of historical importance; its narrow medieval streets and buildings are undergoing a programme of restoration. Places of interest include the seventeenth century church, the château and the remains of the town ramparts. There are several pleasant water fountains in the town.

The famous wooden Virgin of Pradelles, brought back by a crusader, was said to perform a variety of miracles and so attracted a large number of pilgrims. It can be seen, clothed in a white dress, at the far end of the Church (or Chapelle) of Notre Dame at the south end of the town.

The history of the town goes back a long way. In the twelfth century a band of thieves and bandits, under the leadership of one Captain Chambaud, frequently attacked the towns and villages in the area. The day they tried to enter the walled town of Pradelles, they ran into resistance from a peasant woman called "La Verdette"

The church of Notre Dame at Pradelles

(named after the part of the town she lived in). She was so incensed at the assailants that she picked up a stone from the Porte de la Verdette (one of the town gateways) and threw it at the captain, killing him instantly. His men ran off, the woman being declared a heroine. Her famous deed is commemorated in a painting in the Notre Dame church and also in a new stone mural (erected in 1988) in the rue Mazel. Every year for two weeks in July/August the Fêtes Historiques de Pradelles is held, a spectacular pageant in which the history of the town is re-enacted.

For those wishing to stay a while in Pradelles, but still wanting to walk, there is now a new circular walking tour of the surrounding countryside. This is the Circuit Pédestre du Mazonric, the PR125. It is 11.8 miles (19 kilometres) long and is timed at 4 hours 45 minutes. The walk starts from the junction of the D40 and N88 and is waymarked throughout with yellow paint stripes.

Langogne
The town is modern and semi-industrial. The old bridge across the Allier and the covered market are of interest, as is the very fine eleventh century church.

Reservoir de Naussac
Langogne is attracting more tourists these days since the flooding of the wide, fertile Naussac plain after the completion of a dam in the early 1980s. The landscape here, which remained largely unchanged for a century after Stevenson's visit, has now been completely transformed by this artificial lake. The reservoir covers an area of about 1,100 hectares and provides a shoreline some 25 miles (40 kilometres) in length. Anyone staying for a day or more in Langogne may wish to explore further. There is now a waymarked trail around the reservoir, the Tour du Lac (blue and white waymarks). This is tortuous and slow in parts as it negotiates the ups and downs through the woods around the lakeside; in wet weather some areas become very marshy. There are beaches for sunbathing, whilst the more active can swim, windsurf, fish or hire pedalos.

TRAVELS WITH A DONKEY
RLS stayed for less than an hour in Pradelles, omitted to see the

Lady of Pradelles *"who performed many miracles, although she was of wood"*, and was so on *"goading Modestine down the steep descent that leads to Langogne on the Allier —. The long-promised rain was beginning to fall —"* as he crossed the bridge and entered the town. Despite all his problems with Modestine and her heavy burden, and with his incompetent map reading, Stevenson had walked all the way from Le Monastier to Langogne in just two days. This supreme effort was to tell in the days that followed as the pair became more fatigued and travel-weary.

ROUTE

Opposite the Place du Foirail in Pradelles is a larger square, the Place de la Halle (water fountain). Here is a signpost depicting the St Andrew's cross and the Stevenson trail to Langogne. Take the Rue du Mazel downhill under an archway to join the Rue Basse leading to the Chapelle Notre Dame. Continue to the cemetery at the Place Père Charles Boyer. Take the left-hand track (high wall on the left) down to the road (D28), just outside the town. Turn right and follow this road as it bends to the right and then sharply to the left. About 75 yards after passing a road on the right signposted to Le Mazigon and St Clément, turn left on a narrow road signposted Les Bories, Le Mazel and Le Mazonric. In 0.5 mile (0.8 kilometre) do not pass under the railway bridge on the right, but continue ahead to pass a metal cross mounted on a stone plinth and a track on the right leading to Le Mazonric (ignore).

Pass through the hamlet of Les Bories, ignoring tracks to the right and left and remain on the metalled lane heading south. Pass Maison Seule and climb on the road (look back at picturesque Pradelles on the hillside) before entering Le Mazel. Soon after the hamlet the road begins to descend (ignore the small road off to the right). When the road bends to the right Langogne comes into view below. Ignore the track on the right to Le Mas Neuf and descend steeply to the main road (N88). Turn right to cross the river Allier by the road bridge. Pass a large supermarket on the left, pass under the railway bridge (railway station is to the right), turn left for the campsite or keep straight ahead for the centre of Langogne.

LANGOGNE TO LUC VIA CHEYLARD L'EVEQUE

Total distance:		16.4 miles (26.4km)						
Total estimated time:		7hrs 15min						
Map:		IGN 1:50,000 sheet number 2737 (Langogne)						

S = SECTIONAL A = ACCUMULATIVE	Height above sea level		Distance S		A		Est Time S	A
	ft	m	mls	km	mls	km	hr m	hr m
LANGOGNE	3000	915						
ST FLOUR DE MERCOIRE	3413	1041	3.5	5.6	3.5	5.6	1.40	1.40
SAGNE ROUSSE	3868	1180	2.0	3.2	5.5	8.8	1.00	2.40
FOUZILLAC	3868	1180	1.4	2.2	6.8	11.0		
FOUZILLIC	3868	1180	0.3	0.5	7.1	11.5		
CHEYLARD L'EVEQUE	3691	1126	2.1	3.4	9.3	14.9	1.55	4.35
LES PRADELS	3803	1160	2.3	3.7	11.6	18.6		
LUC	3442	1050	4.8	7.8	16.4	26.4	2.40	7.15

FACILITIES

Accommodation

Problems may be experienced on this section in finding permanent accommodation for the night. There is no hotel or *gîte d'étape* in Cheylard l'Evêque and only a small hotel in Luc. There are two other main possibilites:

1. Return to Langogne from Luc by public transport, taxi or by hitching a lift. (Note: The small halt on the railway line at Luc is unmanned but trains regularly stop there.) It is about 10 miles (16 kilometres) between Luc and Langogne along the Allier valley. After staying a second night in Langogne, a return to Luc would have to be made the following morning.

2. Push on to the Trappist Monastery of Notre Dame des Neiges, a further 6.8 miles (11 kilometres) where accommodation may be sought, or to La Bastide-Puylaurant (8.9 miles; 14.4 kilometres)

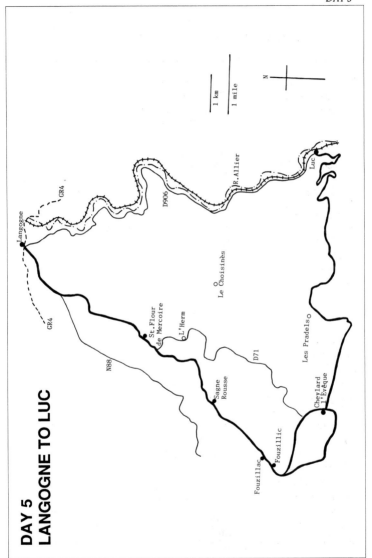

DAY 5
LANGOGNE TO LUC

N

1 km
1 mile

GR4

Langogne

GR4

N88

St. Flour
de Mercoire

L'Herm

Sagne
Rousse

Fouzillac

Fouzillic

Cheylard
l'Evêque

Les Pradels

Le Choisinès

D71

D906

R. Allier

Luc

where there are hotels (see Accommodation - Day 6).

Those walkers carrying a tent will again experience no problems. The municipal campsite (Les Gallets) in Luc is only about 0.3 miles (0.5 kilometres) off-route, down by the river (not marked on the IGN 1:50,000 map). Purists may wish to camp wild - to make *"A Camp in the Dark"* between the hamlets of Fouzillac and Fouzillic!

Restaurants/Cafés/Bars

There is a café in Luc where it may be possible to buy a meal. It is situated down by the river opposite the entrance to the campsite. There are no places of refreshment between Langogne and Luc.

Shops

There is a small but well stocked general store in Luc. This is open even on Sunday mornings. It is passed on route. A mobile baker's van operates in the area, selling both bread and cakes.

THINGS TO SEE; PLACES TO VISIT

Gévaudan

The trail is now entering wildest Gévaudan, where even today there is a feeling of remoteness, not experienced in the Velay. Despite the presence of a (poorly) waymarked route, attention to detail with map and route description will be required if the modern wayfarer is not to experience a similar fate to that of Stevenson who became hopelessly lost in the neighbourhood of Fouzillac (Fouzilhac) and Fouzillic (Fouzilhic). These tiny hamlets are still in existence today, although some of the buildings are in a state of decay. In Stevenson's day the land was exploited by sheep farmers, and as a result of animal over-population, the landscape had become denuded and suffered from erosion. Human depopulation began with the First World War and has continued ever since with the lure of more fruitful work in the towns and cities. In this respect the land is even more remote than it was a century ago. Tourism, particularly rambling, horse and pony trekking and cross-country skiing are going some way towards revitalising the area.

During the 1760s the Beast of Gévaudan roamed this desolate country. Most of the hundred or more killings attributed to the animal took place in the region between Langogne and Luc, the

The Château at Luc

scene of today's walk. The story has it that the king of France himself eventually ordered a huntsman from Paris to track and kill the notorious wolf, which he did with the aid of a silver bullet.

St Flour-de-Mercoire
There is a Romanesque church in the village, together with a rather sad memorial to the men of the district who died during the First World War. It is a world apart from this quiet backwater to the killing fields of northern France.

Cheylard l'Evêque
There is a small chapel (*"the diminutive and tottering church"*), but little else of note in this rather dilapidated village. The old Mercoire Abbey is situated 2 miles (3.2 kilometres) south of Le Cheylard.

Luc
The main item of interest is the massive white Madonna at the ruins of the fortified castle on the hill overlooking the town and valley of the Allier. It is 13 feet (4 metres) high and was dedicated, as Stevenson noted, on October 6, 1878, less than two weeks after his visit. RLS was told that the statue weighed fifty quintals. A dictionary definition of a quintal is a hundredweight, which can be either 112lb or 100lb. However, a Quintal metrique or French quintal equals

100kg, which is equivalent to 220lb avoirdupois. Therefore fifty quintals can be either 5,000lb, 5,600lb, or 11,000lbs!

TRAVELS WITH A DONKEY

Stevenson spent the morning of his third day writing up his journal and it was not until 2.30pm that he set off from Langogne. The weather was poor - "*All the way up the long hill from Langogne it rained and hailed alternatively; the wind kept freshening steadily, — plentiful hurrying clouds — careered out of the north and followed me along my way.*" He reached the hamlet of Sagne-Rousse by 4pm but for the next few hours wandered lost in the fir woods to the south-west. Both the adults and children he encountered gave him no assistance "*He did not care a stalk of parsley if I wandered all night upon the hills!*" At long last, the dusk now rapidly gathering, he arrived at Fouzillic, "*three houses on a hillside, near a wood of birches*". Here he was put on the right course for Cheyland, but soon darkness fell: "*I have been abroad in many a black night, but never in a blacker — the sky was simply darkness overhead — roaring blackness.*"

Stumbling about in the darkness he reached a second hamlet, that of Fouzillac, actually farther from his destination than Fouzillic. He called at a house offering money to pay for a guide to Cheyland, but assistance was refused and he therefore had no alternative but to "*Camp in the Dark*". He was wet from the rain of the afternoon and had neither water, nor bread for himself. His evening meal consisted of one of the tins of Bologna sausages and a cake of chocolate, all washed down with neat brandy!

Despite his deprivations, RLS appeared to have enjoyed the experience. When he awoke "*the world was flooded with a blue light, mother of the dawn — I was surprised to find how easy and pleasant it had been, even in this tempestuous weather. — I had felt not a touch of cold, and awakened with unusually lightsome and clear sensations.*" With assistance from an old man in Fouzillic he was soon "*within sight of Cheylard, the destination I had hunted for so long.*"

He was well received at the inn where he ate, drank and wrote his journal, before setting out for Luc on a road "*through one of the most beggarly countries in the world. It was like the worst of the Scotch Highlands, only worse —.*" It was this section between Cheyland and Luc that promoted him to pen the most famous quote in the book, from which the quote printed at the front of this guidebook is taken. "*Why anyone should desire to visit either Luc or Cheylard is more than my much-inventing spirit can suppose. For my part, I travel not to go anywhere, but to go. I travel for travel's sake. The great affair is to move; to feel the needs and hitches of our life more nearly; to come down off the feather-bed of civilisation, and find the globe granite underfoot and strewn with cutting flints*".

RLS spent the night at Luc, "*a struggling double file of houses wedged between hill and river. It had no beauty, nor was there any notable feature, save the old castle overhead with its fifty quintals of brand-new Madonna*".

ROUTE

Those walkers staying at the one star campsite should follow the GR4 to the High Street in Langogne. From the campsite turn left for about 100 yards and then right to pass under the railway bridge and follow the red/white waymarks along a small lane heading west to reach the river. Here turn left and then right over the first bridge, to reach the High Street, where you turn left. Follow the N88 for about 1.2 miles (1.9 kilometres). There is a pavement on the right hand side of the road until the road-sign is passed indicating the boundary of the town (here turn right if wanting the two star Camping de Naussac). Continue along the N88 (care) passing a track descending to the left to the Pisciculture du Moulin de Marce. About one hundred yards farther on, at the brow of a hill where the N88 swings to the right, bear left off the road onto a track heading south (grand view of wooded hills ahead.)

In about 200 yards ignore the track on the right but continue with the river below on the left. Where the track bends to descend to the left, take an overgrown path on the right (faint blue/white waymarks; also two barbed wires here in August 1990 but these were easy to negotiate). The path soon becomes earthy and stony and leads to the buildings of Barret. Turn to the right and then the left to bend with the track through the buildings and pass underneath the electric wires. A few yards later turn left on a track climbing by the side of a wood. In one hundred yards ignore the left fork. The blue waymarks should now have improved. After a short while as the track swings to the right to continue uphill, take a narrow path off to the left heading west (ie. do not continue on the track to the end of the wood). Follow the path with a brook on the left over barbed wire (easy) to cross an open area (small streams) to reach a stony track on the side of a wood. Ascend on this track (magnetic compass bearing 208°). Leave the wood and continue on a clear track, skirting more woodland at times to reach the church and cemetery at St Flour-de-Mercoire.

At the narrow crossroads by a metal cross, turn right and walk up to the black statue. Here turn left, but after seventy-five yards turn right by another metal cross. Follow this road until it becomes a track when the buildings end. Follow the track to reach a road at a building. Do not walk on this road but keep to an old road to its left. In one hundred yards or so reach a clearing where you take the track ahead climbing towards the trees (ie. ignore the track going left). Follow this track, which is adjacent to the road on its right at first, but soon swings left. Keep to the main track through the wood (note that the white-red-white paint stripes on trees in this area refer to hunting or forestry; they are not waymarks for walkers). At a T-junction of tracks do not turn right or left on the main track, but rather turn sharp right on a narrow path through the wood, heading south-west. This path is soon enclosed by a low stone wall on the left and a fence on the right. Climb over barbed wire (again no problem) and continue through the trees. The route soon becomes a track between barbed wire fences which is followed to a road, where you turn left to enter the hamlet of Sagne-Rousse.

Continue straight ahead (signposted Laubarnès and Cheylard l'Evêque) at the metal cross, but just after the solitary house on the right, take the track off to the right following a line of wooden telegraph poles. In about 150 yards bear right (a blue/white St Andrew's cross). Pass an interesting small stone cross on a boulder in a field on the right and then pass through three barbed wire gates/fences. Continue on a thin path through woodland, on a magnetic compass bearing of 220°. Follow the line of wooden telegraph poles, crossing the Cham brook. Pass through a wooden gate to the right of the poles and climb the small hill beyond on a track. Continue on this track to the road at the hamlet of Fouzillac (perhaps it was not surprising that Stevenson got lost in this area!)

Turn left on the road and continue to Fouzillic. Maintain direction, now on a track, but in about 300 yards turn left (south) on a path passing under telegraph wires. In a further 400 yards at a cross-tracks, there are two alternative routes. Turn left for the direct route to Cheylard l'Evêque or continue ahead for a slightly longer alternative (as described here). After fifty yards bear to the left and left again at a T-junction. Continue on the main track (ignore a track off to the right) to reach a barbed wire gate. Through this and bear left on a track. At a T-junction of tracks turn right and continue to a metalled road where you turn left. The road winds downhill to meet the D71 where you turn right to enter Cheylard l'Evêque.

Turn left on a small road at the metal cross about 50 yards before the church. Cross the Cheylard brook by the road bridge and climb the hill ahead. Ignore tracks at the top of the hill and follow the road downhill. Blue waymarks should be encountered here again; the first time since Sagne-Rousse. Keep to this road down to the Langouyrou brook. Note that although the IGN 1:50,000 map shows this only as a track for much of the way, it has now been surfaced along its entire length. Climb on the narrow lane northwards towards the hamlet of Les Pradels. Just before the village, where the road bends to the left and a track comes in from the right, take a smaller track straight ahead. Where this forks, take the left (lower) branch to reach a road. Turn right and keep to the upper (right) of the two roads ahead. Follow this for several miles all the way to Luc. The narrow road is fringed on either side by a vast array of rosebay willow herbs during the summer. At first the road heads eastwards on a high level plateau and then heads down to the valley by a series of large hairpin loops. There are extensive views of the mountains of the Cévennes that lie ahead. Before descending to the village, turn off to the left to visit the ruins of the Château of Luc, with the *"tall white statue of Our Lady"*, which have been in view for sometime. Reach a T-junction in the village; turn right to continue the RLS Trail (and for the shop; it is fifty yards on the right) or left to descend to the river, campsite and railway.

LUC TO CHASSERADES VIA NOTRE DAME DES NEIGES

Total distance: 16.2 miles (26.1km)
Total estimated time: 7hrs 5min
Maps: IGN 1:50,000 sheet numbers 2737
                        (Langogne) & 2738 (Le Bleymard)

S = SECTIONAL A = ACCUMULATIVE	Height above sea level		Distance S		A		Est Time S A	
	ft	m	mls	km	mls	km	hr m	hr m
LUC	3442	1050						
LE MAS	3442	1050	0.3	0.5	0.3	0.5		
LAVEYRUNE	3216	981	1.1	1.7	1.4	2.2		
ROGLETON	3252	992	1.8	2.9	3.2	5.1	1.20	1.20
LA TRAPPE DE N.D. DES NEIGES	3544	1081	3.7	5.9	6.9	11.0	1.40	3.00
LA BASTIDE PUYLAURENT	3331	1016	2.1	3.4	9.0	14.4	0.55	3.55
LE THORT	3541	1080	2.0	3.3	11.0	17.7		
CHASSERADES	3800	1159	5.2	8.4	16.2	26.1	3.10	7.05

FACILITIES

Accommodation

There are hotels at both La Bastide-Puylaurent (eg. Le Gévaudan, Place de la Gare; Hôtel le Pins, Tel:66.46.00.07) and Chasseradès (eg. Hôtel St Jean, Place de la Gare). The backpacker could elect to stay at the campsite 1.25 miles (2 kilometres) from La Bastide (not marked on the 1:50,000 IGN map, but signposted from the village) which would make for a short day. Alternatively, there is a *gîte d'étape* at L'Estampe, 1.7 miles (2.7 kilometres) past Chasseradès on the RLS Trail (see Day 7). Although accommodation (simple and otherwise) may still be found on request at the monastery of Our Lady of the Snows, it is probably best not to disturb the hard-working monks. There is plenty of other accommodation on this section of the walk.

Restaurants/Cafés/Bars

There are several cafés and restaurants at La Bastide-Puylaurent

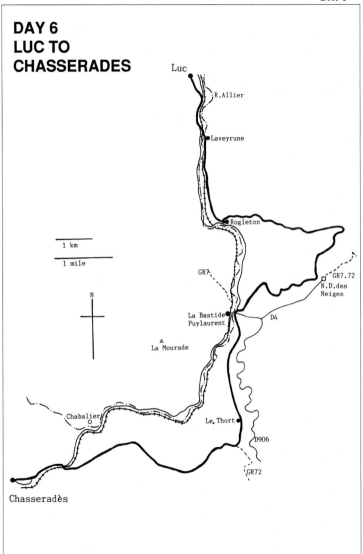

**DAY 6
LUC TO
CHASSERADES**

Luc

R. Allier

Laveyrune

Rogleton

1 km

1 mile

GR7

GR7.72

N.D.des
Neiges

N

La Bastide
Puylaurent

D4

△
La Mourade

Chabalier

Le. Thort

D906

GR72

Chasseradès

and a café at Chasseradès. There is a restaurant near the railway station about a mile before Chasseradès. Refreshments can also be obtained from the buvette at the Notre Dame des Neiges complex.

Shops
La Bastide-Puylaurent boasts several food shops and there is also a store in Chasseradès. Again keep an eye open for mobile grocers and bakers.

Tourist Office
There is a *syndicat d'initiative* in La Bastide-Puylaurent.

Train
La Bastide-Puylaurent, where there is a railway station, is at a junction of two railway lines. (i) The Cévenol route, the main Paris-Nîmes line (north-south). (ii) The La Bastide-Puylaurent to Mende branch line (east-west). On this line there is also a railway station at Chasseradès.

THINGS TO SEE; PLACES TO VISIT
Monastery of Notre-Dame des Neiges (Our Lady of the Snows)
The present monastery complex dates from after 1912, when the buildings visited by RLS were destroyed by fire. Not only the fabric, but also the activities and way of life of the Trappist monks have changed enormously since the 1870s. No longer confined to a life of silence, the monks are now astute businessmen, selling wine, honey, cheeses and souvenirs to the hordes of tourists who are daily disgorged from fleets of tour coaches. There are caves to visit, an audio-visual display on the monastery and the life and work of the inhabitants, a café and, or course, a number of services in the abbey to which the public are welcome to attend. The single rooms for travellers found in Stevenson's day have been replaced by plush accommodation, mainly used by relatives and friends of the monks and others for spiritual retreats.

La Bastide-Puylaurent
There are some interesting stained glass windows in the village and a trout farm nearby; otherwise little of note.

The monastery of Notre-Dame des Neiges

Le Thort
Note the interesting dolmen on the side of the track, about 150 yards past the hamlet.

Ancient Crosses
There are two ancient roadside crosses on the track between Le Thort and Chasseradès, viz. the Croix de Grabio and the Croix de Peyre.

Watershed
The elevated land between La Bastide and Chasseradès is one of the principal watersheds of northern Europe. The Allier flows from one side of it, into the Loire at Nevers and on into the Atlantic, whilst the Chassezac, the stream that runs through Chasseradès, will eventually join the Rhône and so head for the Mediterranean. The head springs of the Allier and the Chassezac lie a mere 150 yards or so apart.

Chasseradès
The twelfth century Romanesque church, built of rough hewn stone, is worthy of a visit.

TRAVELS WITH A DONKEY

Stevenson's half-day from Langogne and enforced encampment near Fouzillac have brought together RLS's itinerary and that described in this guidebook. For the rest of the walk we are to stay 'in front' of Stevenson, finishing one day ahead of his schedule. He was to take several more half-days as he lingered to write up his journal and take prolonged rests. Both RLS and the donkey were suffering from the physical demands of the journey. Modestine in particular was in a very sorry state *"— there were her two forelegs no better than raw beef on the inside, and blood was running from under her tail."*

Stevenson set out from Luc on his fifth day after leaving Le Monastier, having first re-arranged Modestine's saddle-pack yet again. He followed the valley of the Allier, noting that the railway that ran beside the river (the Paris-Nîmes line) was *"the only bit of railway in Gévaudan, although there are many proposals afoot and surveys being made, and — a station standing already built in Mende"*. He was, of course, referring to the branch line from La Bastide to Mende, which is still operational today and which is followed on the RLS Trail from Chasseradès to L'Estampe.

The pair continued along the valley, first to La Bastide where RLS was then directed to *"follow a road that mounted on the left* (the journal erroneously states 'upon my right') *among the hills of Vivarais, the modern Ardèche"*. For a man of Stevenson's Protestant background the Monastery of Notre-Dame des Neiges held unknown horrors. *"I have rarely approached anything with more unaffected terror than the monastery of our Lady of the Snows — fear took hold on me from head to foot."* He first encountered one Father Apollinaris, who escorted him to the gates of the monastery, where, as a literary man, he was graciously received by Father Michael, the father hospitaller. He was wined and dined and spoke with several of the Trappist Monks, who, whilst waiting on a stranger, were allowed the liberty to speak. He was given a guided tour of the monastery by an Irish deacon named Michael O'Callaghan, and attended Compline and Salve Regina at the end of the day, before returning to his spartan room *"clean and whitewashed, and furnished with strict necessities"*. His slumber was disturbed by the first bell of the day at 2am.

Stevenson delayed his departure the next day, discussing politics

'Chaos' boulders on the descent from the Col de Finiels. (Day 8)
The tower on the bridge at Le Pont de Montvert. (Day 8/9). This now
houses an information centre of the Cévennes National Park.

Houses perched precariously above the River Tarn at Le Pont de Montvert. (Day 8/9)

Ridge walking on the GR 68, west of the Col de Planette. (Day 9)

and, even more unwisely, religion with some of the boarders of the monastery. Eventually he was escorted back to La Bastide by his Irish friend, and from there continued along the Allier to Chasseradès, *"a tumbled village on a water course in a bare valley between two bare ranges of hills"*, where he arrived at sunset. He stayed the night at the village inn with five other guests, all of whom were *"employed in survey for one of the projected railroads"*. Politics were discussed until a late hour, when all retired to one stifling room containing four beds. Stevenson, being a gentleman, was allowed a bed to himself.

ROUTE
From the general store in Luc keep to the higher (right) of the two roads to pass through the hamlet of Le Mas. Pass a calvary on the right and descend to the road (N906) where you turn right. Keep the railway to the left and walk south (change from IGN map 2737 to map 2738). Turn left on the D76, signposted Laveyrune. Cross over the railway and then the bridge over the River Allier. Continue, now with the railway line to the right along the D154 passing through Laveyrune and on to the village of Rogleton. Here, about fifty yards before the T-junction and road bridge, turn left on the minor road signposted to Serres. In a few hundred yards, where the road swings to the left, bear right on a track to cross a stream. This track soon becomes rough and stony. Soon take a right (upper) fork, waymarked with yellow/red stripes. Follow these waymarks on the trees to climb through the forest, meeting and following for some way a line of electricity pylons. At the highest point there is an extensive view of the approaching Cévennes mountains: (*"—I beheld suddenly a fine, wild landscape to the south. High rocky hills, blue as amethyst —"*).

Keep to the main track, ignoring side turnings, but just after a small clearing in the wood look out for a grassy path descending to the right on a magnetic compass bearing of 140° (it should be marked with a blue arrow on a tree). The monastery Notre-Dame des Neiges soon comes into view below to the right. Reach a track at a T-junction and turn right and descend on it to the monastery (the track becomes surfaced shortly before the monastery complex). Just below the church turn right at a GR7A signpost (La Bastide). After less than a mile do not turn left to cross the river, but instead go right to follow the road with wooden telegraph poles to the left. Pass to the right of the house ahead on a track and continue to a T-junction of tracks by a pine wood. Here turn left and follow the track past a house on the left to meet a small road at a bend, where you turn left. After a few hundred yards take a path off to the right of this road. Descend this narrow trod to meet buildings on the outskirts of La Bastide. Descend to the church in the village. If wanting to camp turn right here (the three star campsite is two kilometres away.) Otherwise continue straight ahead at the church (signposted Le Thort on the GR72).

After a while the road becomes a dusty forest track. There are superb views of the mountains to the east as Le Thort is approached. Pass through the village (many dilapidated buildings) and continue on the lane signposted GR7A. Pass the partly hidden Croix de Grabio on the right at the top of a hill. Later ignore a track off to the left, but remain on the roughly surfaced road. There are several notices in the area warning of the danger of fire; these woods become tinder-dry during the summer months. About fifty yards after the large Croix de Peyre on the left, leave the road as it swings to the left ie. bear right (straight ahead) on a sandy, grassy track going slightly uphill with a pine wood to the right. Continue on this main track for a couple of miles until another track is met coming in from the left. Bear right here to cross the railway line (beware of trains). Turn left at the road (D6), pass the old railway station and a restaurant and in about 500 yards, where the road bends to the left, bear right on a wide gravel path. This leads directly into Chasseradès.

DAY 7:

CHASSERADES TO CHALET DU MONT LOZERE VIA LE BLEYMARD

Total distance:		11.2 miles (17.9km)						
Total estimated time:		5hrs 5min						
Maps:		IGN 1:50,000 sheet numbers 2738						
		(Le Bleymard) & 2739 (Génolhac)						

S = SECTIONAL A = ACCUMULATIVE	Height above sea level		Distance S		A		Est Time S	A
	ft	m	mls	km	mls	km	hr m	hr m
CHASSERADES	3800	1159						
L'ESTAMPE	3934	1200	1.7	2.7	1.7	2.7	0.50	0.50
LES ALPIERS	3888	1186	4.6	7.4	6.3	10.1		
LE BLEYMARD	3504	1069	1.6	2.5	7.9	12.6	2.25	3.15
COL SANTEL	3934	1200	1.4	2.3	9.3	14.9		
CHALET DU MONT LOZERE	4658	1421	1.9	3.1	11.2	18.0	1.50	5.05

FACILITIES

Accommodation

The first *gîte d'étape* since Goudet (Day 2) is reached at L'Estampe soon after Chasseradès. Note that meals are not provided at this *gîte d'étape*, but there is a well-equipped kitchen and hot showers. There is a second *gîte d'étape*, 0.6 mile (1 kilometre) off-route at Le Mazel south of Le Bleymard, and the stage finishes at the *gîte d'étape* on Mont Lozère. Hence those who have not so far sampled this unique French style of accommodation, now have plenty of opportunity to do so on this section of the walk.

Walkers preferring more luxurious accommodation have the choice of the hotel in Le Bleymard (La Remise, Tel:66.48.65.80) or the two star hotel on Mont Lozère. Le Bleymard, a popular ski resort in winter, used to boast up to three hotels until the early 1990s and it is possible that more will be opened here again in the future.

Campers are again spoilt for choice. There is a small *Camping à*

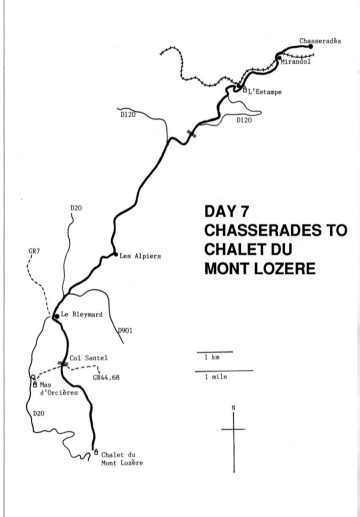

Chasseradès

Mirandol

L'Estampe

D120

D120

D20

GR7

Les Alpiers

**DAY 7
CHASSERADES TO
CHALET DU
MONT LOZERE**

Le Bleymard

D901

Col Santel

GR44.68

Mas
d'Orcières

D20

1 km

1 mile

N

Chalet du
Mont Lozère

la Ferme site in L'Estampe (new in 1988) and the trail passes the campsite in Le Bleymard. Camping is also permissible at the end of the stage on Mont Lozère.

Restaurants/Cafés/Bars
There are several restaurants and cafés in Le Bleymard. At the Mont Lozère ski-complex there are two bar/restaurants.

Shops
Le Bleymard has *épiceries* and a *boulangerie*.

Public Transport
A bus service operates between Villefort (railway station), Le Bleymard, Bagnols-les-Bains and Mende (railway station). It operates once each way on Wednesdays and Fridays only, and on Sunday evenings during school term.

The modern railway network is left at L'Estampe and is not encountered again on the remainder of the journey to St Jean du Gard.

THINGS TO SEE; PLACES TO VISIT
Mirandol
The massive curving railway viaduct dominates the view. This, and the remainder of the line to Mende, was being surveyed at the time of Stevenson's visit. Notice the slate tiles *(lauzes)* on the roofs of the houses in the village.

L'Estampe
Note the swallowhole beside the road just above the hamlet (marked G^{fre}, for "Gouffre," on the 1:50,000 IGN map). There are many more swallowholes on the limestone plateau of the Causse de Montbelle above Belvézet, to the north-west of L'Estampe.

Le Goulet (4,908 feet; 1,497 metres)
The first major climb of the walk and the start of the Cévennes mountains. Once out of the trees on the descent, the views are extensive. The RLS Trail reaches a high point of 4,632 feet (1,413 metres), but the actual summit (viewpoint) can be reached by a detour of about 1.5 miles (2.4 kilometres) to the west.

Les Alpiers

Signs of depopulation are evident in the rather run-down slate houses. Many have now been sold as holiday homes. Note the small primitive cross by the roadside.

Le Bleymard

This pleasant town, which has a number of interesting old houses, is now a thriving ski-resort, owing its popularity to the vicinity of Mont Lozère, ideal for both downhill and cross-country Ski de Fond.

River Lot

The trail crosses the River Lot at Le Bleymard, only a few miles from its source in the foothills of the Cévennes, to the north-east of Les Alpiers.

TRAVELS WITH A DONKEY

RLS was woken at the inn at Chasseradès at daybreak, 5am, and was soon on his way to L'Estampe and from there climbed to the southwest over the Montagne du Goudet. He was in good spirits, believing that he was "— *now done with rains and winds and a bleak country*". This was a significant point on his journey. He was now, at long last, entering the Cévennes. "*The first part of my journey ended here; and this was like an induction of sweet sounds into the other and more beautiful.*"

On "*springy and well scented*" turf, and with "*no company but a lark or two*" he descended into the shallow valley of the Lot, beyond which he observed the range of the Lozère, "*sparsely wooded and well enough modelled in the flanks, but straight and dull in outline*".

Stevenson lunched in Le Bleymard before goading Modestine up through the woods towards Mont Lozère, where he found a "*dell of green turf, where a streamlet made a little spout over some stones to serve me for a water-tap*". Here he spent "*A Night among the Pines*" greatly enjoying the scents, sounds and sights of a starry night on the mountain. Although delighting in his own company he was obviously missing Fanny Osborne, for he wrote: "*to live out of doors with a woman a man loves is of all lives the most complete and free.*" He was to write later that *Travels with a Donkey* was full of "*mere protestations to F*". He so enjoyed the night in the open air, that he

Unloading the donkey outside the gîte d'étape at l'Estampe

decided to leave some payment, "— *to leave pieces of money on the turf as I went along, until I had left enough for my night's lodging".*

ROUTE

Turn left in front of the church in Chasseradès and follow the GR7A signpost indicating a *gîte d'étape.* Go past a cemetery on the left and descend to the railway line, where you turn left to pass under a viaduct. At the road (D6) turn right to enter Mirandol (impressive gorge on left). Pass under the viaduct and immediately turn sharp left on a path to pass back underneath the viaduct. In a few yards turn right and back under the viaduct again. Turn left to pass under the viaduct yet again with a stream on the right. Pass over a bridge and ascend the lane ahead. At the top of the short climb turn right over slabs and in a few yards bear left. Ascend on a track to a cross-tracks where you turn right, descend, cross a small brook and re-ascend with the railway line over to the right. Reach and follow the railway line (below to the right) to the lane at L'Estampe. Turn left to enter the village (*"The narrow street of Estampe was full of sheep, black and white all bleating and tinkling the bells around their necks".)* Note that

103

this route from Mirandol to L'Estampe is not shown on the 1:50,000 IGN map, but the route is clear and easy to follow.

Pass the *gîte d'étape* on the right, then a small rural campsite and climb gently on the road (D120) with views to the wooded mountains ahead. The road bends as it climbs, but about one hundred yards before it enters the trees, turn right on a track which itself soon reaches trees. Pass through a gate and take the left fork ahead on a grassy path. In fifty yards take the right (lower) fork and one hundred yards later the left fork. Remain on the main track as it climbs steadily through the trees, ignoring minor tracks to the right and left, until it eventually reaches the road again where you turn right. Remain on the road when it levels out but where it bends sharply to the right (signposted 'Le Bleymard 8') take the track straight ahead (signposted Les Alpiers and C.D.901, Pont du Lot).

In fifty yards take the track bearing to the right. This slowly descends through the forest. After less than a mile take the left-hand track at a fork and in a further mile turn right following a wide path to the left of a wood. Descend to a track where you turn left to enter Les Alpiers. Walk down between the dilapidated buildings, bearing to the right and turn right by a concrete telegraph pole. Notice the interesting, small, primitive cross on the right. Remain on the main track, ignoring a track on the left in about a quarter of a mile. However one hundred yards later where the track divides, take the left fork (Le Bleymard seen in the valley below). About sixty yards farther on take the right hand of three tracks (green/white sign with deer symbol). This soon becomes a narrow path which descends through Christmas trees to the D901 road opposite a campsite. Turn right and enter Le Bleymard.

Turn left off the main road (signposted Le Bleymard Centre, D20). In about 250 yards turn left at the monument to Henri Rouvière (a French anatomist) on the rue de Couderc. At the top of the small hill take the left of three small roads. At a small metal cross and concrete bench at a bend in the road, turn right on a track (the old drove road, or *draille*). In fifty yards ignore the upper path which veers off to the left, but keep on with the building below right. Climb this grassy track, descend slightly to a T-junction at a sandy track and turn right, continuing to Col Santel. Here is a division of paths. Left leads on the GR44/68 to Cubières in forty-five minutes, and right is the path for the GR68 and the *gîte d'étape* at Le Mazel. Ahead lies the GR7, coincident with the RLS Trail (signposted to the Col de Finiels). Climb through the forest heading for the mast seen ahead. After a few hundred yards of climbing bear left by a green/white sign with pine tree symbol. This grassy track climbs less steeply at first, but later it resumes its original steepness as it becomes more stony. Follow more green/white pine tree signposts at a number of path junctions, climbing to meet a line of telegraph poles (change from IGN map 2738 to map 2739).

The track reaches its high point and then gently descends, still following the telegraph poles and with glorious views of the Cévennes mountains. Continue to an open area and eventually reach the Chalet du Mont Lozère. This unattractive complex has a number of buildings: a station du ski, chalets, bar/restaurant with combined *gîte d'étape* - 'Le Refuge', and a two star hotel and bar/restaurant opposite.

The primitive stone crucifix
at Les Alpiers

CHALET DU MONT LOZERE TO LE PONT DE MONTVERT
VIA LE COL DE FINIELS

Total distance:	9.8 miles (15.8km)		
Total estimated time:	3hrs 50min		
Map:	IGN 1:50,000 sheet number 2739 (Génolhac)		

S = SECTIONAL A = ACCUMULATIVE	Height above sea level		Distance S		A		Est Time S A	
	ft	m	mls	km	mls	km	hr m	hr m
CHALET DU MONT LOZERE	4658	1421						
COL DE FINIELS	5075	1548	2.7	4.3	2.7	4.3	1.20	1.20
FINIELS	3967	1210	3.4	5.5	6.1	9.8	1.10	2.30
LE PONT DE MONTVERT	2868	875	3.7	6.0	9.8	15.8	1.20	3.50

FACILITIES

Accommodation

Le Pont de Montvert has accommodation of all types. There are hotels, (eg. Hôtel Aux Sources du Tarn. Tel:66.45.80.25) a *gîte d'étape* and a campsite.

Restaurants/Cafés/Bars

There are several such establishments at Le Pont de Montvert, but there is little opportunity for refreshment between the Chalet du Mont Lozère and Le Pont de Montvert (crêpes may be on sale at the hamlet of Finiels).

Shops

Food can be bought in a number of shops in Le Pont de Montvert. The small town also possesses a bank.

Tourist Office

There is a *syndicat d'initiative* in the Le Pont de Montvert. There is also a Cévennes National Park information centre housed in the tower on the bridge at Le Pont de Montvert.

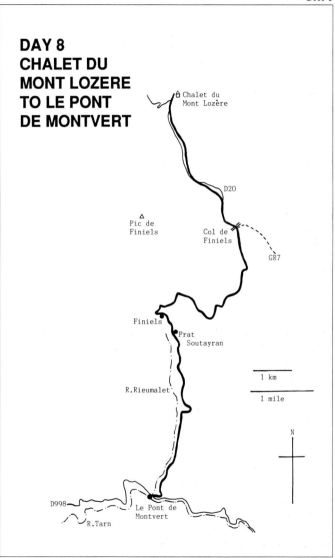

**DAY 8
CHALET DU
MONT LOZERE
TO LE PONT
DE MONTVERT**

Chalet du
Mont Lozère

D20

△
Pic de
Finiels

Col de
Finiels

GR7

Finiels

Prat
Soutayran

1 km

R.Rieumalet

1 mile

N

D998

Le Pont de
Montvert

R.Tarn

Public Transport
There is an infrequent bus service that passes through Le Pont de Montvert destined for Florac. Details from the *syndicat d'initiative.*

THINGS TO SEE; PLACES TO VISIT
Mont Lozère
The Col de Finiels on Mont Lozère, at 5,075 feet (1,548 metres) is the highest point reached on the standard route of the RLS Trail, and the only time that the 5,000 foot mark is exceeded. The Pic de Finiels (5,570 feet; 1,699 metres) itself, is the highest point on Mont Lozère and in the Cévennes; indeed only the volcanic *puys* of Mont Dore and Cantal in the Auvergne and Mont Mézenc in the Velay exceed it in height in the whole of the Massif Central. The view is extensive; even the Mediterranean can be seen on a clear day.

Drove Roads - Drailles
There are many ancient drove roads or *drailles* in the Cévennes, some of which are still used to drive sheep or cattle along to market. These old tracks often provide the best and easiest walking through the rugged, stony and scrub-covered hills; the RLS Trail uses many of them on its way south to St Jean du Gard. *Drailles* are particularly evident on Mont Lozère, where they are often marked with a line of standing stones called *montjoies*. Ancient boundary stones engraved with Maltese crosses may also be found on the ridges of Mont Lozère.

Chaos
On the descent from the Col or Pic de Finiels to the village of the same name, several large piles of granite blocks and boulders will be seen. These are called *'chaos'* in French; the English equivalent would be 'tors'. Very photogenic.

Finiels
There is an annual 'Fête of the Myrtilles' (bilberries) held in August in this small mountain village.

Le Pont de Montvert
A most picturesque Cévenol town located at the confluence of three rivers, the Tarn, Rieumalet and Martinet. There are many fine sixteenth century houses built on rocks above the waters, along
108

'Chaos' granite boulders on Mont Lozère (Pic de Finiels)

narrow winding streets, but the most attractive feature of the village is possibly the seventeenth century humped-back bridge over the River Tarn, with its old toll tower, now an information centre of the Cévennes National Park. There is also an "Ecomusée du Lozère" (ecological museum) nearby, open during the main summer months.

It was in Le Pont de Montvert that the war of the Camisards broke out in 1702. Events leading to this particularly vicious and bloody struggle for religious freedom began with the issuing of the Edict of Nantes by Henry IV of France in 1589, granting religious toleration to French Protestants. However, the edict was revoked by Louis XIV in 1685, the practice of the austere Protestant faith being forbidden by the Catholic authorities. As a result some 400,000 French Protestants (Huguenots) fled the country for the more religiously tolerant states of northern Europe; many settled in England. Although many left from the Cévennes, these were a hard mountain people who resisted the attempt of the state to rid the area of Protestantism and enforce the alien Catholic faith on the population. Local representatives of the Catholic authorities, together with troops billeted on the residents were used to coerce the people into the Catholic faith. Protestantism was practised in secret, usually in caves or fields, and most of the pastors went into hiding, preaching,

109

baptising, marrying and burying the dead in secret. The Catholic authorities were responsible for many atrocities, and torture, imprisonment, deportation and execution were commonplace. The Catholic governor of the district around Pont de Montvert was the Abbé (or Archpriest) du Chayla, notorious for personally torturing his Protestant prisoners which he kept in the cellars of his riverside house. This house is no longer there, having been re-built as a grocer's/souvenir shop, but the cellars can still be seen.

One night in 1702, the Abbé du Chayla was brutally murdered at Le Pont de Montvert by a gang of fifty-two men, this event sparking off the guerrilla War of the Camisards, which continued for much of the ensuing century, until the revolutionary Government of 1789 granted religious freedom to the French Protestants. Esprit Séguier, the leader of the killing, was caught within a few days and burnt alive. Catholic churches were burnt and their priests murdered, as the populance organised themselves into a small guerrilla army under the leadership of Roland and Jean Cavalier. The Protestants became known as the Camisards after the shirts ('camisa' in the old tongue, Occitan) which distinguished them from the French army dressed in uniform and armour. Fearful retribution followed, the king's army burning hundreds of Cévenol villages and massacring the inhabitants. All this had a devastating effect on the landscape, still much in evidence today, with a low, scattered population living in small, wall-enclosed villages. At the time of Stevenson's visit in 1878, the Camisard War was just within living memory.

The injustices went deep; even today there are separatist organisations and slogans may occasionally be seen in Occitan. When visiting the Protestant chapel and the Catholic church in Le Pont de Montvert, it is well to bear in mind the events of the eighteenth century in this once troubled region.

TRAVELS WITH A DONKEY

Stevenson was in high spirits during the morning he spent on Mont Lozère, enjoying the sunshine and extensive views of the high Cévennes. On reaching the highest point on his entire journey on the Pic de Finiels he was moved by the *"confused and shaggy country"* at his feet and the *"undecipherable labyrinth of hills"*, declaring that these are *"the Cévennes of the Cévennes"*. One of the reasons for his journey was to visit the land of the Camisards, the French equivalent of the Scottish Covenanters, and on crossing the Lozère he wrote that he *"— had travelled through a dull district,"* but that now *he "— was to go down into the scene of a romantic chapter — in the history of the world"*.

RLS followed a line of ancient marker stones to the top of the Pic de Finiels and then a track corkscrewing *"into a valley between falling hills, stubbly with rocks like a reaped field of corn, and floored further down with green meadows"*. He descended quickly: *"The whole descent is like a dream to me, so rapidly was it accomplished,"* seeing *"not a human creature,"* until *"the Tarn at Pont de Montvert of bloody memory. — The place, with its houses, its lanes, its glaring river bed, wore an indescribable air of the South."*

ROUTE

From the complex of buildings on Mont Lozère proceed to the D20 road where you turn left to enter the Parc National des Cévennes. In seventy-five yards bear left, just before a modern chapel on the right, onto a brown, surfaced road. Pass under a ski lift and climb on this road which follows the line of the modern D20, but remains below it. After about 0.5 mile (0.8 kilometres) bear left off this surfaced road onto a grassy track. This route is that of the old drove road or *draille*. Pass under another teleski and in twenty yards bear right on the higher track. This soon becomes a narrow path with a fence on the left. This path eventually fords a stream and re-joins the road. Turn left and continue uphill on a path to the left of the road with a fence to the left. A little later cross over the road and take a stony track, now with the road over to the left. On joining the D20 again continue uphill to the Col de Finiels, the highest point on the road at 5,075 feet (1,548 metres).

The route described above is the most straightforward and the only one to follow in mist, heavy rain or other adverse conditions. However, for those with mountain walking experience, it is also possible, in good weather, to follow a route, marked in places by a line of tall, granite guidestones ('*Monts-Joie*' or '*Montjoies*') to the Sommet of Finiels' (5,570 feet; 1,699 metres). This route avoids the Col de Finiels and emerges on the D20 road about 0.5 mile (0.8 kilometres) before (north-east) and above the hamlet of Finiels.

For those wishing to take this mountain alternative the following description is provided. The use of the IGN 1:25,000 map is useful here and spot heights mentioned in the description refer to this map.

From the Chalet du Mont Lozère proceed south on the D20 but after about 200 yards fork right and soon right again on a grassy ascending track which leads to a low stone building. Here turn right on a wide track which contours south, then west to a wood, and then south again to reach a stone refuge hut near point 1,529 metres (marked as 'Refuge' on the 1:50,000 map). About 500 yards after the refuge, cross a culvert over a stream and after a further one hundred yards (at the last of the conifers on the right) turn left uphill on a magnetic compass bearing of 210° (no path visible on the ground) to reach the top of the ridge and a small cairn at 1,685 metres. Turn left here along the ridge (120°) to follow a line of cairns to the Sommet de Finiels at 1,699 metres (the ridge is actually a broad plateau, the highest point being marked by a rusty iron structure). From the Sommet descend slightly and re-ascend (75°) to point 1,688 metres, then descend again (115°) to a junction of tracks at a col at 1,635 metres. Take the grassy track downhill (due south) past several tall granite posts. This path descends through trees, first to the left and later to the right of a stream in a deepening gully. The path is narrow but well used and always easy to follow. Reach the D20 at a bridge over a stream (point 1,312 metres). Turn right and follow the road down to the hamlet of Finiels.

To continue on the standard route. At the Col de Finiels ignore the track off to the left (the GR7) but instead remain on the D20. The winding road continues over the plateau until, emerging from the woods, a glorious mountain panorama opens of rocky ridges and distant blue mountains. There are a number of large boulders in a variety of curious formations to be seen close to the road in this area. On this descent a good view is provided of Mont Finiels with the hamlet of Finiels nestling below.

At Finiels there are two alternative routes. It is possible to follow a path which starts from near the cemetery in Finiels and heads south, to the west of the River Rieumalet, to the hamlet of Rieumal. The route is not an easy one to follow and there are numerous gates and fence obstructions to negotiate. From Rieumal take the "white" road which first heads north-east and later turns to the south, joining the D20 half a mile before Le Pont de Montvert. The other, more straightforward route follows the D20 south down the Rieumalet valley. The superb views will do much to relieve any discomfort experienced from the hard surface underfoot. Pass through the hamlet of Prat Soutayran, later ignoring the left turn to L'Hôpital, continuing down this most impressive valley to the junction with the D998. Turn right to enter Le Pont de Montvert, pass a St Andrew's cross marker on the left and turn left over the stone bridge over the River Tarn.

LE PONT DE MONTVERT TO FLORAC
VIA LE COL DE LA PLANETTE

Total distance: 14.8 miles (23.8km)
Total estimated time: 6hrs 50min
Maps: IGN 1:50,000 sheet numbers
                       2739 (Génolhac) & 2639 (Florac)

S = SECTIONAL A = ACCUMULATIVE	Height above sea level		Distance S		A		Est Time S	A
	ft	m	mls	km	mls	km	hr m	hr m
LE PONT DE MONTVERT	2868	875						
COL DE LA PLANETTE	4236	1292	3.9	6.2	3.9	6.2	2.10	2.10
COL DU SAPET	3606	1100	3.7	6.0	7.6	12.2	1.40	3.50
MONTAGNE DE LEMPEZOU	3062	934	5.5	8.9	13.1	21.1		
FLORAC	1790	546	1.7	2.7	14.8	23.8	3.00	6.50

FACILITIES

Accommodation

Florac offers a variety of hotels (eg. Grand Hôtel du Parc. Tel:66.45.03.05) as well as a *gîte d'étape*. There are two campsites at Florac. There is another possibility of accommodation at the *gîte d'étape* in the hamlet of Mijavols, a thirty-minute detour off-route, roughly half way between Le Pont de Montvert and Florac.

Restaurants/Cafés/Bars

These are to be found in abundance in Florac although there is no opportunity for refreshment en route between Le Pont de Montvert and Florac.

Shops

Florac has shops of all types as well as a bank and post office.

Tourist Office

Florac has a *syndicat d'initiative* (Avenue Jean Monastier). The town is also the headquarters for the Cévennes National Park and provides information on all activities within the park.

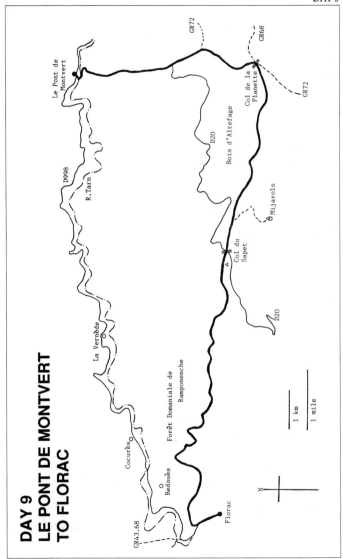

DAY 9
LE PONT DE MONTVERT
TO FLORAC

GR72

GR68

Le Pont de Montvert

Col de la Planette

GR72

D20

Bois d'Altefage

D998

R.Tarn

Mijavols

Col du Sapet

La Vernède

D20

Forêt Domaniale de Ramponenche

Cocurès

1 km

1 mile

N

Bedouès

GR43.68

Florac

Public Transport

A bus (once daily in each direction) operates between Florac and Alès, stopping at Florac, St Julien-D'Arpaon, Cassagnas, Jalcreste, St Privat-de-Vallongue, St Hilaire-de-Lavit, Le Collet-de-Dèze, Ste. Cecile-d'Andorge (railway) and Alès.

THINGS TO SEE; PLACES TO VISIT

GR68

The RLS Trail follows the GR68 for about ten miles from the Col de la Planette to Florac. This is arguably the most scenic part of the entire journey. Much of the route follows a high ridge with extensive views of the wooded hillsides and deep-cut valleys of the Cévennes mountains. There are interesting ancient standing stones on the Col du Sapet and the route passes through the Bois d'Altefage, the wood from which the first operation of the Camisards' War was launched.

Tarn Valley

Those following Stevenson's route down the D998 will see the fourteenth century Château de Miral on a rocky point above the river. The fortified church at Bédouès is also worth a visit.

Florac

A most attractive town situated at the foot of the high limestone cliffs of the Rocher de Rochefort, at the confluence of the Rivers Tarn, Tarnon and Mimente. It lies at a point where permeable limestone meets impermeable schists, and this leads to the re-appearance of a subterranean stream, the Source de Pêcher, which flows through the centre of the town down a series of terraces. The seventeenth century château is worth a visit; it was fortified during the War of the Camisards. Many of the streets are delightful, being shaded by avenues of plane trees. Stevenson stayed the night at an inn in rue Thérond, Florac. Being close to Mont Lozère, the southern Cévennes, Causse Méjan (a superb limestone plateau) and the Tarn Gorges, Florac is an excellent centre for a future holiday, either walking, horse/pony riding or car touring.

Tarn Gorges

The spectacular Tarn Gorges are situated farther down the River Tarn, between Ispagnac (twelfth century church and castle) and Sainte-Énimie, west of Florac. A visit is highly recommended. A day

Florac, situated beneath the limestone cliffs of the Rocher de Rochfort

would have to be set aside for this. An infrequent bus service from
Florac, heading towards Mende may be a help, but it is also worth
enquiring at the *syndicat d'initiative* as tourist bus tours sometimes
operate during the main season. Finally, it may be possible to hire
a bicycle in Florac, so allowing a visit to the gorges. Look out in the
town for signs indicating 'bicycles for hire' or ask at the *syndicat
d'initiative*.

TRAVELS WITH A DONKEY

RLS had lunch at the inn at *"Pont de Montvert, or Greenhill Bridge"*
where he ate in the company of three women and flirted with the
waitress. He left the village on *"a new road —from Pont de Montvert
to Florac by the valley of the Tarn, a smooth sandy ledge"*. Today this is
the busy D998 metalled road. His spirits were still high as he
journeyed beneath the chestnut trees, *"— from bays of shadow into
promontories of afternoon sun"*. A short way down the valley he
sought out a small *"unpleasantly exposed"* plateau above the road, to
where he *"goaded and kicked the reluctant Modestine"* and camped for
the night. Stevenson was by now enjoying his nights under the stars,
in fine and warm weather, although on this occasion he was

117

bothered by rats who made disturbing sounds, *"such a noise as a person would make scratching loudly with a finger nail"*. He was thus less pleased with his lodgings than on the previous night on Lozère and so declined to leave any payment in his usual manner, but nevertheless gave money to a beggar-woman he met the following morning.

After making his *"morning toilette in the water of the Tarn"*, he continued down the valley making several acquaintances on the way, including a 'Plymouth Brother' with whom he discussed religion and accompanied to the hamlet of La Vernède, *"a humble place, with less than a dozen houses, and a Protestant chapel on a knoll"*. He took breakfast at the inn where he discovered that the villagers *"— were all Protestants - a fact which pleased me more than I should have expected"*.

After resting awhile with these friendly and *"upright and simple"* folk, he continued his journey, visiting the ruins of the Château de Miral and passing through Cocurès, *"sitting among vineyards and green meadows and orchards"*, followed by Bédouès, where he saw *"a battlemented monastery long since disabled and turned into a church"*. And so he arrived in Florac, *"as perfect a little town as one would desire to see — with an old castle, an alley of planes, many quaint street-corners, and a live fountain welling from the hill"*. He spent the afternoon and night at an inn in the town where he conversed with the locals and was given advice on the route for the next (and last) stage of his journey to St Jean du Gard. He observed that *"Protestant and Catholic intermingled in a very easy manner"*, but was *"surprised to see what a lively memory still subsisted of the religious war"*.

ROUTE

From the stone bridge over the River Tarn in Le Pont de Montvert, turn left, pass the entrance to the campsite and leave the town on the D20. Head south on this for nearly two miles (3.2 kilometres) to a point where the road bends sharply to the right (west). Here take the forest track which leaves the road just before the bridge over the Torrent du Valet de la Tour. This pleasant track, the Sentier des Cols du Bougès, is signposted with a green/white waymark carrying the symbol of a black rabbit. Some care is required on the next section as the route is easily lost. On reaching a small clearing locate a blue sign indicating the route over to the right, to cross a stream by a small concrete bridge and take a track heading west. Pass a small metal hut on the right and soon after reach a dusty track where you turn sharp left (south - south-east). Pass buildings on the right and where the track bends to the left, continue ahead (signposted GR72 - Crête du Bougès). Climb steeply through the forest, remaining on the main track, ignoring side tracks to the right and left. Eventually emerge at cross-tracks on the Col de la Planette (4,236 feet; 1,292 metres).

For those short of time a day can be saved here by following the G72 south from the Col de la Planette. The route is clearly seen on the IGN 1:50,000 maps. Take the track marked on the map as a single black line. This meets a "white road" which is followed south to the Col du Poulio and from here to a second Col de la Planette. Follow the winding road down to Cassagnas and the Mimente valley. It is about 5.3 miles (8.5 kilometres) from the first Col de la Planette to Cassagnas.

However, for those not pressed for time, the standard route to Florac on the GR68 is recommended. The blue RLS Trail waymarks stop from this point onwards. Bear right at the Col de la Planette on a good track heading for a mast, following the red/white flashes of the GR trail. Shortly, on reaching a clearing, follow a green/white/black rabbit sign to a GR68 arrow. Bear left to follow this, climbing to a large cairn (4,583 feet; 1,398 metres). Descend to a road, emerge from the trees and climb on the open ridge ahead. Pass the Signal du Bougès (4,658 feet; 1,421 metres) and continue on a clear path along the ridge with a wood to the right. There are extensive views. Pass through a section of woodland, continue on the open ridge and reach a signpost indicating the way to the *gîte d'étape* at Mijavols down to the left. Remain on the ridge, passing through sparse woodland and scrub on a narrow, sandy and rocky path to reach the road (D20 again) at the Col du Sapet (3,606 feet; 1,100 metres).

Cross the road and follow the broad track ahead, eventually entering the Forest of Ramponenche. At a crossing of tracks (five tracks) go straight on, soon passing a small stone shelter on the left. Turn left at a T-junction where the orange signposted bridleway leaves the GR68. Later at a clearing where the track turns sharply to the left, look for a narrow path off to the right (no waymark at this

119

point, but one should soon be found if the correct path is taken). The path descends gently through woodland and scrub and soon Florac and the valley below come into view. Care is required here as the path becomes indistinct in places. Head towards the west aiming for a small ruined stone building, from where a path leads downhill. Descend to a fence, pass over a stile (of sorts; the only one on the entire trail) and descend on a path through trees (change from IGN map No.2739 to No.2639). Farther down be sure to take a small path off to the left of the main track (this is just before the track divides). Emerge on the N106 at the Pont de la Bessède over the River Tarnon. Here will be seen the first signpost indicating St Jean du Gard! Turn right for the *gîte d'étape* or for one of the campsites. But to continue on the RLS Trail, cross the bridge and enter the town of Florac.

FLORAC TO CASSAGNAS VIA ST JULIEN D'ARPAON

Total distance:	11.4 miles (18.5km)	
Total estimated time:	5hrs 15min	
Maps:	IGN 1:50,000 sheet numbers 2639 (Florac), 2739 (Génolhac) & 2740 (St André de Valborgne)	

S = SECTIONAL A = ACCUMULATIVE	Height above sea level		Distance S		A		Est Time S	A
	ft	m	mls	km	mls	km	hr m	hr m
FLORAC	1790	546						
BALAZUEGNES	2459	750	6.0	9.7	6.0	9.7	3.00	3.00
ST JULIEN D'ARPAON	2000	610	0.4	0.6	6.4	10.3	0.15	3.15
LE VIVIER	2262	690	4.6	7.4	11.0	17.7	1.50	5.05
CASSAGNAS (LE STEVENSON)	2272	693	0.4	0.6	11.4	18.3	0.10	5.15

FACILITIES

Accommodation

This stage of the walk terminates at the small *gîte d'étape (relais d'étape)* which occupies the old railway station near Cassagnas in the Mimente valley. Meals are available at the Relais Stevenson. Note that this *gîte* has room for only six occupants. If walking during the main summer holiday period it might be advisable, if possible, to phone ahead to book a place for the night. The only real alternative is to combine Days 10 and 11 to form a very long walk to St Germain-de-Calberte. Note that Cassagnas village has no hotel, café or shop.

Campers have the choice of two stopping places: at the campsite at St Julien d'Arpaon or at the small campsite near the *gîte d'étape* and "Le Stevenson" Bar-Restaurant. Neither campsites are marked on the IGN 1:50,000 map.

Restaurant/Cafés/Bars

There is a café at St Julien d'Arpaon, but most walkers on the RLS Trail will be making for the Bar-Restaurant "Relais Stevenson" (Tel:66.45.20.34) located at the end of today's stage.

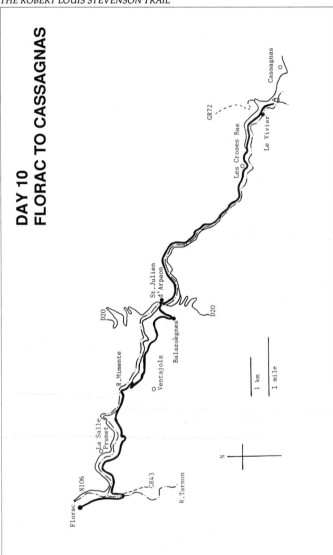

DAY 10
FLORAC TO CASSAGNAS

Shops

It is advisable to stock up on provisions at Florac, as no shops will be passed on this section. A small selection of supplies may be available at the café or campsite at St Julien d'Arpaon (again keep a watch for mobile grocers' or bakers' vans).

Public Transport

See under Day 9.

THINGS TO SEE; PLACES TO VISIT

Mimente Valley

The steep sided Mimente valley is most impressive. Stevenson noted in his journal: *"— steep rocky red mountains plunged down upon the narrow channel of the Mimente, their edges eaten by the rains and winds into a fantastic and precarious lacework —"*.

The Mimente Railway

The second disused railway on the RLS Trail can be followed with benefit for part of the way between Florac and Cassagnas. The history of the line is of interest. When the French railway network was being designed during the heyday of European railways, a decision was made by the French authorities to provide all *Sous-Préfectures* (in addition to *Préfectures*) with a railway station and connecting railway. However, Florac (*Sous-Préfecture* of the Lozère department) posed a problem, as the mountainous terrain made it impractical to route the Paris-Clermont Ferrand-Nîmes line via Florac. The government of the day therefore granted financial assistance to the local railways (Chemin de Fer Départemental) so that a single, metre-wide track could be built from Florac to Ste Cécile d'Andorge to join up with the main line. It was built during the late 1880s (ie. after Stevenson's visit) using predominantly local labour to dynamite a passage for the line, construct the several tunnels required and lay the sleepers. The line carried both passengers and freight (mainly wood, certain minerals and lead from the Col de Jalcreste). However, the parallel road in the Mimente valley had already been constructed (many new roads were being built at the time of Stevenson's visit) and with the advent of motorised transport, the line, which was a slow one, proved unpopular. It was eventually closed in 1948.

Château de Montvaillant

This is located on the opposite (north) bank of the River Mimente, half a mile to the east of Florac.

St Julien d'Arpaon

The castle ruins at St Julien d'Arpaon are referred to by Stevenson, "—one (hamlet) *with an old castle atop to please the heart of the tourist*". In 1617 the owner, one Jacques de Gabriac, was executed for robbery of royal salt tax collectors and the castle was destroyed. It was later re-constructed but only the southern and eastern walls remain .

Cassagnas

There is little to see in the actual village which now has a permanent population of little more than twenty people.

TRAVELS WITH A DONKEY

The rigours of their long trek were taking effect as Stevenson and Modestine left Florac late in the afternoon of the first day of October, *"a tired donkey and tired donkey-driver"*. RLS had once again spent the morning catching up on his journal and resting. The pair did not get far that day, but soon made camp in the Mimente valley, on what was to prove their last night together out in the open. Stevenson was impressed with the rocky grandeur of the valley but the steepness of the terrain posed problems for a suitable campsite. He eventually found a spot close to the river and mused on the beauty of the starlit sky: *"No one knows the stars who has not slept, as the French happily put it, à la belle étoile — ignorant — of their serene and gladsome influence on the mind."*

Stevenson was awoken the next morning by the barking of a dog from a nearby house, and was soon on his way up the valley. He met only one other traveller *"a dark and military-looking wayfarer"*, that morning on his walk to Cassagnas. *"I was now drawing near to Cassagnas, a cluster of black roofs upon the hillside, in this wild valley, among chestnut gardens, and looked upon in the clear air by many rocky peaks."* It is noticeable that in the later stages of his journey RLS, as he became more fatigued, made fewer entries into his journal at the time. Considerable sections were added at a later date when he was preparing the manuscript for *'Travels with a Donkey'*. However, even in the latter, relatively little is written on the final few days from Florac to St Jean du Gard.

ROUTE

Leave the town of Florac on the D907 heading south down the valley of the Tarnon (return to IGN map No.2739). Ignore the first road bridge over the Tarnon (unless requiring the campsite, which is on the opposite bank of the river at this point) but continue on the minor road signposted GR43 Col des Faïsses two and three-quarter hours. Cross the Tarnon by the picturesque Pont de Barre, thereby leaving the GR43. Note that there are neither red/white GR waymarks nor blue RLS Trail signs from here until Cassagnas. Immediately after crossing the bridge, turn left up a path heading north above the river. On reaching a track turn right (east) to walk above the River Mimente. At a surfaced road by a small bridge turn left (orange waymark). There is dramatic rock scenery over to the left. In a few hundred yards turn right again (another orange waymark). Continue to follow these orange signs, ignoring a track on the left. The walker soon looks down on the village of La Salle-Prunet on the opposite bank of the river.

After about a mile leave the surfaced road by taking a dirt track off to the left (orange 'hoof print' waymark). Note that an old route of the RLS track, ie. that suggested in the bilingual centenary guide and in the Topo sheet, remained on this road to the hamlet of La Borie, and then crossed over to the village of Ventajols on the opposite hillside. High fences across the hillside have now made this route impassable. Therefore, take the dirt track mentioned above. After about 0.5 mile (0.8 kilometres) ignore a track climbing up to the right (waymarked as orange route No.5), but continue on the track to reach the N106 road where you turn right. This could be followed all the way to St Julien d'Arpaon but the road is busy and unpleasant. Instead, leave the N106 after about 0.3 mile (0.5 kilometres) by turning sharp right on a narrow lane (wooden signpost Ventajols). Take the hairpin bend to the left, but at the next bend (a right-hand one) walk ahead on a narrow path to the right of a small ruined building. The route is a little indistinct in places but should present no real problems. The path maintains direction (magnetic compass bearing 114°) through trees and after a while is

The Relais Stevenson, near Cassagnas

accompanied by a fence on the right. Eventually after more than a mile (1.6 kilometres) it emerges onto open hillside (glorious view) and the path then becomes more distinct, soon reaching the buildings of Blazuègnes. Walk on a track between the houses to the small road, where you turn left to descend back to the main road.

Turn right on the N106 and walk into the village of St Julien d'Arpaon. Cross the bridge over the Mimente. Walk past the old railway station house and through the campsite, to follow the old railway track to the left of the river. Notice the old sleepers buried in the track. Pass under two railway tunnels (the second bends to the left and is somewhat dark, but no torch is necessary) and over two bridges, eventually reaching the main N106 road at Maillautier. Turn left on the road (change from IGN map No.2739 to No.2740). About one hundred yards after the turn on the left to Les Croses Bas take a track off the road down to the right. Pass a house on the left and continue with the river on the right. Pass Le Vivier and just after a sign indicating the Gare de Cassagnas and café in 350 metres pass a water tap and small campsite on the right. The first blue RLS Trail waymark since the Col de la Planette, south of Le Pont de Montvert, will soon be encountered.

DAY 11:

CASSAGNAS TO ST GERMAIN DE CALBERTE

Total distance:		9.3 miles (15.0km)						
Total estimated time:		4hrs 45min						
Map:		IGN 1:50,000 sheet number 2740 (St André de Valborgne)						

S = SECTIONAL A = ACCUMULATIVE	Height above sea level		Distance S		A		Est Time S A	
	ft	m	mls	km	mls	km	hr m	hr m
CASSAGNAS (LE STEVENSON)	2272	693						
LE PLAN DE FONTMORT	2937	896	2.7	4.4	2.7	4.4	1.30	1.30
COL DE LA PIERRE PLANTEE	2921	891	4.1	6.6	6.8	11.0	2.00	3.30
ST GERMAIN DE CALBERTE	1574	480	2.5	4.0	9.3	15.0	1.15	4.45

FACILITIES

Accommodation

There is a *gîte d'étape* and a hotel (Le Petit Calbertois, Tel 66.45.93.58) at Le Serre de la Can, about 0.5 miles (0.8 kilometres) to the north-west of St Germain-de-Calberte. There is also the Hôtel Serre de Lacan, 1.2 miles (2 kilometres) before St Germain. As today's section is only a short one some walkers may prefer to continue for a few more miles along the trail. Another *gîte d'étape* will be found 4 miles (6.4 kilometres) past St Germain-de-Calberte at the Pont de Burgen, and a little more than 3 miles (4.8 kilometres) after this at Le Martinet, south of St-Étienne Vallée-Francaise, is a hotel-bar restaurant and a nearby campsite.

Restaurant/Cafés/Bars

St Germain-de-Calberte has a restaurant and a couple of café/bars.

Shops

There are three grocers' shops in St Germain-de-Calberte (one is a small supermarket). There is a *boulangerie,* a *charcuterie* and honey is also for sale in the village. There is a bank in St Germain but it is only open for two hours on Saturdays.

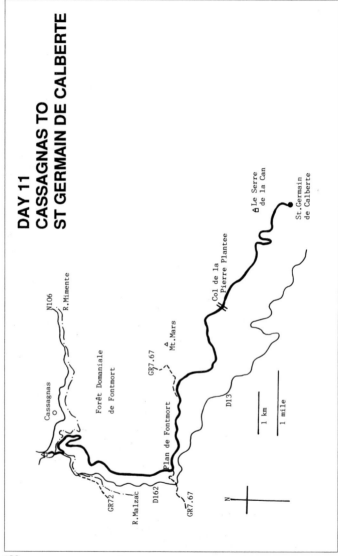

DAY 11
CASSAGNAS TO
ST GERMAIN DE CALBERTE

The River Tarnon near the Pont de Barre on the outskirts of Florac.
(Day 10)

'Travels with a donkey'. A wayfarer with heavily laden donkey on the RLS
Trail near St Germain de Calberte. (Day 11)

Madame Pat Valette of Club Cévenol on the RLS Trail near St Etienne Vallée-Francaise. The St Andrew's Cross indicating the RLS Trail is above the red and white GR waymark. (Day 12)

St Jean du Gard, the end of the trail. (Day 13) *Photo: J-P Vriet*

Tourist Office
There is both a *syndicat d'initiative* and a Centre d'Information du Parc National des Cévennes in St Germain-de-Calberte.

Public Transport
See under Day 9.

THINGS TO SEE; PLACES TO VISIT

Le Plan de Fontmort (Font Morte)
Here is a monument to the Camisards' Revolt, erected in 1887 (ie. after Stevenson's visit). It was here, according to RLS that *"Poul with his Armenian sabre slashed down the Camisards of Séguier"*.

Menhirs
There are several ancient standing stones along the route, in particular at the Plan de Fontmort, the Col de la Pierre Plantée (as the name suggests) and, on the alternative route, at the Col des Laupies.

Watershed
The hills between the Mimente valley and St Germain-de-Calberte form an important watershed. Behind, all the streams and rivers flow eventually into the Garonne and so on to the Atlantic or *"Western Ocean"*. Ahead, the waters drain into the Rhône and thence to the Mediterranean.

Mont Mars (3,809 feet; 1,162 metres)
The summit and viewpoint of Mont Mars can be reached by a detour from either the standard or the alternative route to the Col de la Pierre Plantée.

Forest
The whole area is heavily forested. This is in sharp contrast to Stevenson's day when centuries of 'transhumance', the movement of tens of thousands of animals from lowland to upland pasture, had stripped the land of vegetation and topsoil. A policy to plant trees and so combat the erosion was implemented by a government official, Georges Fabre, in 1875. As can now be witnessed, this afforestation programme was highly successful.

Chestnut trees, much admired by RLS, are common on the hillside of the Cévennes. In the sixteenth century the chestnut was the staple diet of the population and even in Stevenson's day was an important source of food and income. They were eaten fresh, in soups or stews, or were dried and ground into flour for bread (the 'tree of bread'). No part of the tree was wasted: the wood was used to build furniture, the inner bark for basket making and the foliage was fed to the livestock.

The hillsides hereabouts are dotted with numerous caves used as hideaways by the Camisards in the eighteenth century and later by the resistance fighters during the Second World War.

Le Serre de la Can
This is a horse riding centre and stud farm. There is accommodation and stabling facilities and holidays can be taken hacking the numerous marked trails in the area.

Saint Germain-de-Calberte

A pleasant southern mountain town which remained Catholic during the Camisards' War. There are plane trees in the small square and flowers decorate the many terraced gardens. The twelfth century Romanesque church has an interesting decorated doorway. The Abbé du Chayla, whose murder started the War of the Camisards (see Le Pont de Montvert), is buried inside the church.

TRAVELS WITH A DONKEY

Stevenson had lunch at the inn in Cassagnas in the company of *"a gendarme and a merchant"*, the latter considering Stevenson's journey to be foolhardy and dangerous. RLS approved of the villagers who *"seemed intelligent after a countrified fashion, and were all plain and dignified in manner"*.

"A little after two" Stevenson left Cassagnas and *"struck across the Mimente and took a rugged path southward up a hillside covered with loose stones and turfs of heather"*, marvelling at *"perhaps the wildest view of all my journey"*. He traversed the Col des Laupies and was directed to the road for St Germain-de-Calberte by a very old shepherd, who mistook Stevenson for a pedlar. On the descent he was overtaken by nightfall but was assisted by a bright moon (*"purified nocturnal sunshine"*) until this went behind a hill and he pursued his way *"in great darkness"*. He entered St Germain-de-Calberte which was *"asleep and silent, and buried in opaque night"*, and stayed the night at the village inn.

ROUTE

From the Stevenson Café take the GR72 to cross the Mimente by an iron bridge. In a few hundred yards bear left on a track, leaving the GR72 at a St Andrew's cross. Go over a bridge and keep to the main track as it climbs first to the north, then south, then north and finally south again. Later ignore a track on the left and continue ahead (west). In a further 400 yards ignore a track descending to the right. The pleasant woodland path climbs gently until it reaches a small clearing (extensive views to the right) and then descends a little to a cross-track, to the east of Le Plan de Fontmort. Here there is a GR7-67 sign, an orange "horseshoe" waymark and a St Andrew's cross. Turn left on the track going down hill.

This track is the old road to St Germain-de-Calberte and presents fine views of the distant 'blue' mountains. In about 1.5 miles (2.4 kilometres) the path divides. The GR7-67 (E4) goes to the left (Col de Jalcreste) but the RLS Trail takes the right fork to follow the GR67A signposted St Germain-de-Calberte. Continue on this clearly defined track, along which the scent of pine trees is intoxicating, to reach the Col de la Pierre Plantée where there is a junction of four paths. Take the second left (GR72A) at a St Andrew's cross, to descend to another junction of paths, where you turn left (signposted Serre de la Can Piste). In seventy-five yards turn sharp right on the GR67A. Eventually emerge from the trees to see St Germain-de-Calberte below to the left. Descend on a zig-zagging path to a road, where you turn right to enter the village (———"*I was shot without pre-paration into Saint-Germain-de-Calberte*").

There is an alternative route to that given above, which in fact follows more closely the trail taken by Stevenson between Cassagnas and St Germain-de-Calberte. However, it does include a section of road walking along the busy N106. The route can be clearly seen on the 1:50,000 IGN map. Head east from Cassagnas going downhill to join the N106 and follow it for 0.5 mile (0.8 kilometre) until a path can be taken down to a footbridge over the River Mimente. Join the disused railway and follow it eastwards to the old station at Le Pradal. Here climb towards the south on an old drove road to the Col des Laupies. Continue south along the ridge on a 'white road' to the Col de Pierre Plantée, where the standard route described above is joined to St Germain-de-Calberte.

ST GERMAIN-DE-CALBERTE TO ST JEAN DU GARD
VIA ST ETIENNE-VALLEE-FRANCAISE

Total distance:	15.2 miles (24.6km)
Total estimated time:	7.00hrs
Map:	IGN 1:50,000 sheet number 2740
	(St André de Valborgne)

S = SECTIONAL A = ACCUMULATIVE	Height above sea level		Distance S		A		Est Time S	A
	ft	m	mls	km	mls	km	hr m	hr m
ST GERMAIN DE CALBERTE	1574	480						
PONT DE BURGEN	898	274	4.0	6.4	4.0	6.4	1.40	1.40
ST ETIENNE-VALLEE-FRANCAISE	836	255	2.9	4.6	6.9	11.0	1.10	2.50
LE MARTINET	787	240	1.0	1.6	7.9	12.6	0.25	3.15
COL DE ST PIERRE	1957	597	2.4	3.9	10.3	16.5	1.30	4.45
SOMMET DE ST PIERRE	2278	695	0.1	0.2	10.4	16.7	0.15	5.00
COL DE ST PIERRE	1957	597	0.1	0.2	10.5	16.9	0.10	5.10
PIED DE COTE	688	210	2.3	3.7	12.8	20.6	1.00	6.10
ST JEAN DU GARD	623	190	2.4	3.9	15.2	24.5	0.50	7.00

FACILITIES

Accommodation

There is a *gîte d'étape* at the Pont de Burgen, north of St Etienne-Vallée-Française and another at St Jean du Gard at the end of the trail. At Le Martinet there is a hotel on the River Gardon de Ste. Croix, and St Jean du Gard offers a wide range of hotels (eg. L'Oronge).

There is a pleasant campsite by the river south of St Etienne-Vallée-Française. It is marked on the 1:50,000 map (Fabrègue) but it does not advertise its presence and can be a little difficult to locate (ask at the house just after the sharp bend to the south on the D983 east of Le Martinet). There is a water tap but no other facilities are provided. There are two campsites (Mas de la Cam and Le Petit Baigneur) along the D907 on the last stages of the trail into St Jean

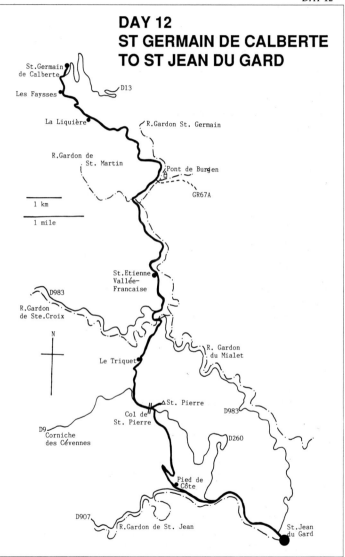

**DAY 12
ST GERMAIN DE CALBERTE
TO ST JEAN DU GARD**

St.Germain de Calberte

Les Faysses

D13

La Liquière

R.Gardon St. Germain

R.Gardon de St. Martin

Pont de Burgen

GR67A

1 km

1 mile

St.Etienne Vallée-Francaise

D983

R.Gardon de Ste.Croix

N

R. Gardon du Mialet

Le Triquet

△St. Pierre

D983

Col de St. Pierre

D9
Corniche des Cévennes

D260

Pied de Côte

D907

R.Gardon de St. Jean

St.Jean du Gard

du Gard. Several campsites will be found in the vicinity of St Jean du Gard; the nearest is probably Les Sources, north-north-east of the town on the D50, about 0.6 mile (1 kilometre) from the centre. The latter has a restaurant-bar and swimming pool. There is also a *camping à la ferme* at Mas Dunal 0.8 mile (1.3 kilometre) from St Jean du Gard.

Restaurants/Cafés/Bars
These can be found in St Etienne-Vallée-Française and in great abundance in St Jean du Gard.

Shops
St Etienne-Vallée-Française has several food shops, a bank (open only on Tuesday afternoons) and a post office. There are shops of all kinds in St Jean du Gard and several banks. There are gift shops if a souvenir or present is sought at the end of the holiday, but better selections will be found in Alès and at Nîmes.

Tourist Office
There is *syndicat d'initiative* in St-Etienne-Vallée-Française and a principal *office de tourisme* in St Jean du Gard (Place Rabaut).

Public Transport
There are two buses a day between St Jean du Gard and Alès via Mialet and Luziers, operated by Cars Fort. These run every day, except Sundays and fête days, during July and August. There is also a service to Alès via Anduze, operated by Lafont Tourisme. This runs three times daily, again during the main summer holiday season. An inferior service operates for the remainder of the year. There are also buses to St André-de-Valborgne via Saumane and to Nîmes via Anduze and Lézan. These services all leave from the *gare routière* (coach park) opposite the office de tourisme in St Jean du Gard, from where up-to-date timetables and further information can be obtained. Finally a tourist steam train runs from St Jean du Gard railway station (south of the river) to Anduze during the summer season. A bus may then be taken from Anduze to Alès for the train home.

THINGS TO SEE; PLACES TO VISIT
St Etienne-Vallée-Française
The château overlooking the river and the ancient bridge are the

main items of interest. There is an old beacon tower between St Etienne-Vallée-Française and Le Martinet.

Corniche des Cévennes
The high mountain road linking Barre-des-Cévennes at the Col des Faïsses to St Jean du Gard. Built as a military road during the reign of Louis XIV, it is a considerable feat of engineering.

St Pierre (2,278 feet; 695 metres)
There is a superb viewpoint from the *table d'orientation* on the summit. The wooded hillsides of the Cévennes stretch, seemingly endlessly, to the north, whilst the valley of the Gardon, journey's end, lies far below. A time for reflection.

TRAVELS WITH A DONKEY
RLS stayed the morning in St Germain-de-Calberte, a *"little Catholic metropolis, a thimblefull of Rome, in such a wild and contrary neighbourhood"*, claiming that he had *"— not often enjoyed a place more deeply"*. However, his thoughts were elsewhere: *"Perhaps someone was thinking of me in another country."* He was missing Fanny Osbourne terribly and longed to reach Alès where he hoped for news from her.

Stevenson dined and took coffee with two Catholics and as a result did not leave St Germain-de-Calberte until *"—long past three"*. Nevertheless he was determined to reach St Jean du Gard without an intermediary stop. The couple passed through St Etienne-Vallée-Française, *"or Val Francesque as they used to call it; and towards evening began to ascend the hill of St Pierre"*. Modestine was goaded without mercy on this *"long and steep ascent"* because he *"dearly desired to see the view upon the other side before the day had faded"*. However, it was dark by the time they reached the summit (presumably the col) where they ate their last meal together. The outline of Mont Aigoual was clearly visible in the moonlight as the pair made the *"long descent upon St Jean du Gard"*. He arrived in the town very late at night: *"Before ten o'clock we had got in and were at supper; fifteen miles and a stiff hill in little beyond six hours!"*

Stevenson had originally intended to continue on foot to Alès. Soon after leaving Le Monastier, when having problems in persuading Modestine to follow the trail, he had declared that: *"The thought that this was to last from here to Alès nearly broke my heart."* However, he was impatient to reach Alès for his letters, and when

135

Modestine was declared unfit for travel on the following day, he decided to sell the donkey and take the stage-coach to Alès. Modestine was sold, *"saddle and all"* for 35 francs, considerably less than he had paid for the donkey. She lived in happy retirement for several years with the man who bought her from RLS and is buried in a field in St Jean. The inn-keeper back in Cheylard L'Evêque had told RLS that before a few days he *"— should care to love Modestine like a dog"*. And so it seemed as he wept for the animal on his journey to Alès. *"For twelve days we had been fast companions; we had travelled upwards of a hundred and twenty miles, crossed several respectable ridges, and jogged along with our six legs by many a rocky and many a boggy by-road."*

ROUTE
Walk through St Germain-de-Calberte on the D984 and bear right at a fork signposted Pont de Burgen, Nouveau Trace GR67A. About 300 yards after leaving the village on the D984 take a marked track off to the right (signposted Les Faïsses 200m gauche). In 200 yards ignore the path off to this establishment, but continue to climb on the track ahead. When this bends sharp right go ahead on another track to meet and cross a road (St Andrew's cross and sign to St Etienne VF). Descend on the main track passing several houses, with good views to the left. Go ahead at a cross-tracks. After descending somewhat by a series of zig-zags with a house on the left, remain on the main track, ignoring side turnings. About 400 yards after swinging left on the track at a rubbish tip, bear right off the main track at a St Andrew's cross and red/white marker. Some 400 yards later look out for markers indicating a narrow path on the left leading down to a road. Cross this, bearing half left to descend a steep, narrow path through trees to another small road. Turn left here for the *gîte d'étape* at the Pont de Burgen, reached in 300 metres on the GR67A. Turn right for the RLS Trail.

Follow the narrow lane to the D984 at a hairpin bend. Turn left, cross the bridge over the river and continue on the D984 with the river to the left. After about 0.5 mile (0.8 kilometres) take a grassy track leading off to the right, which climbs above and runs parallel to the road. Where this track ascends to the right, follow the path ahead (view of river down to the left). Meet a track at a hairpin bend and take the left fork descending, soon ignoring a grassy track descending to the right. After passing a building on the left, descend to the road where you turn right to walk into St Etienne-Vallée-Française.

Head south through the village on the D984, continuing to its junction with the D983, where you bear left (signposted St Jean du Gard). Cross the bridge over the Gardon de Ste. Croix at Le Martinet (Hotel-Bar Restaurant) and immediately turn right up a path (blue and white arrow). The path climbs on zig-zags at first and then maintains a direction of 208° (magnetic bearing). After a final steep section on this stony path, reach a track where you turn right, continuing to climb steadily. This eventually emerges on the D9 (the Corniche of the Cevénnes) at which point the climb is virtually over. Turn left ascending gently to reach the Col de St Pierre.

From the col there are two alternative routes to St Jean du Gard. Whichever trail is taken, a path should first be followed to the summit of St Pierre. Leave the road at the col, climbing to the north-east on a path waymarked with blue and white stripes. This leads to the summit where there is a *table d'orientation* and a superb all-round view of the mountains of the Cévennes (recommended). For the standard route to St Jean, return to Col St Pierre.

Just below the Col St Pierre locate a path marked Pied de Côte St Jean (ignore the earlier path waymarked with a blue/white arrow, Les Cabriérous No.2). Descend steeply at first on a rocky path waymarked with both blue RLS Trail waymarks and with blue/white signs, indicating a local footpath. Descend passing a building on the right and a house on the left (L'Affenadou) where you turn right on a descending track. Follow this drove road which descends first to the north and later to the south to reach the D907 at Pied de Côte. Turn left along the D907 following this road alongside the River Gardon all the way into the centre of St Jean du Gard, where you may wish to light a candle in the church to mark the end of your pilgrimage.

The alternative route to St Jean du Gard starts from the summit of St Pierre at the *table d'orientation.* The route is waymarked with blue-white-blue paint stripes and leads down to the village of Arbousse and then down to the valley at St Jean du Gard. It has the advantage of avoiding the final D907 road section into St Jean du Gard.

DAY 13:

ST JEAN DU GARD AND ENVIRONS. ALES, NIMES

The Last Day

Stevenson did not stay long in St Jean du Gard (— *"I was now eager to reach Alais* (Alès) *for my letters —"*) but those who have followed his journey south from Le Monastier would be well advised, if time is still available, to relax after the labours of their walk and spend some time in the neighbourhood before returning home. St Jean du Gard is a pleasant southern town whose motto, in the old Occitan language is 'Al Sourel de la Liberta - in the sunlight of freedom'. The attractions of the area include the following:-

1. The ancient town ramparts, clock tower and old bridge across the River Gardon.
2. The steam railway. Steam trains run from the railway station in St Jean du Gard to Anduze, from May to September on Thursdays, Fridays and Sundays. Some of the locomotives are British-made.
3. Musée des Vallées Cévenoles (Cévenol Valleys Museum) Housed in a seventeenth century *auberge,* the museum deals with all aspects of Cévenol life including chestnut culture and the old silk industry. Open daily from June to September, except Mondays and Sunday mornings.
4. The Musée du Désert at Mas Soubeyran. This is just beyond Mialet (bus, fifteen minutes from St Jean du Gard; *gîte d'étape*) on the D50. The house, situated amongst rather austere mountain scenery, is where the Camisard leader Roland (Pierre Laporte) was born. It now houses an exhibition depicting the traditional life style of the Cévenol people and outlining the Protestant struggle of the eighteenth century, some of which is so vividly described by Stevenson. The names of many of those who lost their lives in the Camisard War are written on the walls in gold lettering. Recommended.
5. Provided the walker has not been, like Modestine *"pronounced unfit for travel"*, there are a number of local walks that can be taken to explore the country around St Jean du Gard. These are

The River Gardon at St Jean du Gard

clearly waymarked with blue-white-blue paint stripes and are from one to several hours in duration. Details from the tourist office. Those looking for something more ambitious are recommended to take the circular Tour des Cévennes, the 81-mile (130 kilometres) GR67 which can be joined at Mialet to the east or at the Col de Ascliér to the west, by following the GR61 from St Jean du Gard (see Appendix Two). A French Topo guide to the walk can be purchased locally.

If time is available then a trip to Nîmes can be recommended. The city can be reached from St Jean du Gard either directly by bus (about one and a half hours) or first bus to Alès and then by mainline train. Nîmes is rich in antiquities, the main attraction being the magnificent amphitheatre in the centre of the city. Other places of interest include the Maison Carrée (Roman temple and museum), Temple of Diana, Roman bathhouse and ornamental gardens (Quai de la Fontaine), Porte d'Auguste (Roman gateway), Tour Magne (watchtower) and the Museum of Old Nîmes. There is a youth hostel (Tel:66.23.25.04) in Nîmes, as well as many hotels of all categories.

APPENDIX ONE:

GITES D'ETAPE ON OR IN THE VICINITY OF THE RLS TRAIL

1. **Le Puy en Velay**
   Youth hostel. Centre Pierre Cardinal. Rue Jules Vallès. Near the cathedral. Sixty-two places. Meals available. Tel 71.05.52.40
2. **Goudet**
   Gîte d'étape de Goudet. Twenty places. Meals available.Tel 71.57.18.05
3. **L'Estampe**
   Gîte d'étape de l'Estampe. 1.7 miles (2.7 kilometres) south-west of Chasseradès. Twenty-three places. Tel 66.46.01.41
4. **Le Mazel**
   Gîte d'étape Le Mazel. 1.5 miles (2.4 kilometres) to the south of Le Bleymard. Twenty places. Open between April and October. Tel 66.48.61.38
5. **Mont Lozere**
   Gîte d'étape du Mont Lozère, "Le Refuge". Thirty-six places. Meals available. Tel 66.48.62.83 or 66.47.62.83
6. **Le Pont de Montvert**
   Gîte d'étape de Pont de Montvert. Maison du Mont Lozère. Thirty-two places. Meals available. Tel 66.45.80.10
7. **Mijavols**
   Gîte d'étape de Mijavols. About 1 mile; 1.6 kilometres (and 300 metres of descent) off-route. South of the Col du Sapet, approximately mid-way between Le Pont de Montvert and Florac. Twenty places. Meals available. Tel 66.45.09.04
8. **Florac**
   Gîte d'étape de Florac. Rue de la Tannerie. Nineteen places. Meals available. Tel 66.45.56.96 or 66.45.02.03
9. **Cassagnas**
   At the site of the old railway station in the Mimente valley (not in the village of Cassagnas). Six places. Meals available. Open from May to November. Tel 66.45.06.53 or 66.45.20.34
10. **Le Serre de la Can**
    About 0.5 mile (0.8 kilometres) to the north-west of St Germain de Calberte. Forty places. Meals available. Tel 66.45.91.83
11. **Pont de Burgen**
    Between St Germain de Calberte and St Etienne-Vallée Française. Fifteen places. Meals available. Tel 66.45.73.94
12. **St Jean du Gard**
    Gîte d'étape du Moulinet. On the road to Lasalle (D153). Fifteen places. Meals available. Tel 66.85.10.98

There are several other *gîtes d'étape* in the Velay, Gévaudan, Vivarais and Cévennes, but all some distance from the RLS Trail. Full details of all the *gîtes d'étape* in the area will be found in the book *Gîtes d'étape de Randonnée et Refuges* by Annick and Serge Mouraret (see Bibliography).

APPENDIX TWO:

FURTHER DETAILS OF THE GR TRAILS ENCOUNTERED ON THE RLS TRAIL

GR3 *Sentier de la Loire*
600 miles (966 kilometres) or more of footpaths following the course of the River Loire from the sea in Brittany, near St Nazaire, to its source close to the Gerbier de Jonc, south-east of Le Monastier-sur-Gazeille. The route passes through the following regions: Océan, Brière, Anjou, Val de Loire, Orléanais, Niverais, Bourbonnais, Forez and Velay. Gentle, attractive and varied terrain. The GR3 is encountered on the RLS Trail between St Martin de Fugères and Goudet.

GR 40 *Tour du Velay*
100 miles (161 kilometres) encircling Le Puy. The itinerary includes Vorey, Mont-Bar, Allègre, Siaugues St Romain, La Durande, Montbonnet, Le Bouchet St Nicolas, Goudet, Alleyrac, Les Estables, Mont Mézenc, St Front, Boussoulet, Mont Meygal, Le Pertius and St Julien du Pinet. Guidebook in preparation (Alan Castle and Cicerone Press - see Bibliography).

GR4 *Sentier Méditerranée - Océan*
A very long west to east route from Royan on the Atlantic coast to Grasse above the Côte d'Azur. The route passes through the following regions: Océan, Saintonge, Limousin, Auvergne, Margeride, Cévennes, Vallée du Rhone, Gorges du Verdon and Provence. It crosses the RLS Trail at Langogne. A guidebook to the Auvergne section from Volvic to Langogne is in preparation (Alan Castle and Cicerone Press - see Bibliography). A guide is also being planned to the Provençal section of the route (same author and publisher).

GR7 *Sentier Vosges - Pyrénées*
Another ultra-long distance route stretching from Ballon d'Alsace to Andorra in the Pyrenees. On the way the route passes through the Vosges, Plateau de Langres, Côte d'Or, Mâconnais, Beaujolais, Lyonnais, Vivarais, Cévennes, Haut Languedoc, Corbières and Pyrenees. The GR7A, which is followed by the RLS Trail, is a variant of the GR7 running between La Bastide-Puylaurent and Le Bleymard.

GR44

A 54-mile (87 kilometre) spur of the GR4, running west from Les Vans on the GR4 to Villefort, Mas d'Orcières, Col de la Loubière and Champerboux. The route passes just to the south of Le Bleymard where it crosses the RLS Trail.

GR68 *Tour du Mont Lozère*

A circular walking tour, 68 miles (110 kilometres) in length, encircling the mountain massif in the southern Auvergne. From Villefort on the Paris-Nîmes railway line, the route includes Cubières, Orcières, Col des Sagnoles, Florac, Croix de Berthel, L'Aubaret, Gourdouse and Les Bouzèdes. Much of this is within the Cévennes National Park. The RLS Trail follows the GR68 for over 10 miles (16 kilometres) between the Col de la Planette and Florac.

GR43 *La Draille de la Margeride*

A 55-mile (88 kilometre) route following an ancient drove road linking the GR4 at Sainte Eulalie to the GR7 at the Col des Faïsses, west of Barre des Cévennes. It is a harsh trail, passing through uninhabited country with little opportunity, with the exception of Florac, of finding accommodation. The route is coincident with the RLS Trail through Florac.

GR72

The GR72 links the GR4 near Le Bez to the GR7 at the Barre des Cévennes. It is followed on the RLS Trail for the 2 miles (3.3 kilometres) between La Bastide-Puylaurent and Le Thort, and is met for a second time at the Maison Forestière de Champ-Long de Bougès, to the south of Le Pont de Montvert. From here it is followed for a short distance to the Col de la Planette, where the RLS Trail leaves the GR72 to head west to Florac on the GR68. However, the GR72 could be taken as a short cut from the Col de la Planette to Cassagnas, thereby omitting the large loop to Florac on the RLS Trail. The GR72 and the GR72A (a variant) are also encountered for a short distance between Cassagnas and St Germain de Calberte.

GR67 *Tour des Cévennes*

An 81-mile (130 kilometre) walking tour encircling the valleys of the numerous Gardon rivers. From Anduze the trail heads to St Felix de Pallières and Colognac and over the Col de Asclié and the Col du Pas to Aire de Côte, east of Mont Aigoual. The path continues to L'Hospitalet, Barre des Cévennes, Plan de Fontmort, Col de Jalcreste and then south to St André de Lancize, Mialet, Mas Soubeyran and back to Anduze. It is followed on the RLS Trail for a couple of miles from the Plan de Fontmort, south of Cassagnas.

GR67A

A variant of the GR67. It leaves the main route 2 miles (3.3 kilometres) to the west of the Plan de Fontmort and heads south-east to St Germain de Calberte. It crosses the River Gardon St Germain at the Pont de Burgen before re-joining the GR67 near St Martin de Boubaux. It is followed by the RLS Trail for 8.6 miles (13.8 kilometres) from the point at which it leaves the GR67 to the west of the Plan de Fontmort to the Pont de Burgen, north of St Etienne-Vallée Française.

GR61

A short trail linking two points on the GR67, viz. Mialet, north of Anduze and the Col de Asclié, north-west of Colognac. In so doing it passes through St Jean du Gard where the RLS Trail terminates.

E4

Sections of the GR7, GR72 and GR44 form part of the European Long Distance Path which runs from Rust in eastern Austria, across northern Switzerland and southern France to Fredes, south-west of Barcelona in Spain, a distance of 2,122 miles (3,414 kilometres). The E4 passes through the Cévennes National Park from Vans to Villefort to Mont Aigoual and then on through the Haut-Languedoc Regional Park, still following the GR7.

APPENDIX THREE:
STEVENSON'S ITINERARY

1st Day. Sunday September 22, 1878
LE MONASTIER SUR GAZEILLE — ST MARTIN DE FUGERES — GOUDET (lunch) — USSEL — LE BOUCHET ST NICOLAS
Overnight in an *auberge* at Le Bouchet St Nicolas

2nd Day. Monday September 23, 1878
LE BOUCHET ST NICOLAS — PRADELLES (lunch) — LANGOGNE
Overnight at inn (?) in Langogne

3rd Day. Tuesday September 24, 1878
Started after lunch ie. 2.30pm (morning spent writing journal).
LANGOGNE — FOUZILHIC/FOUZILHAC
RLS lost his way in the dark. He camped out overnight, *"A Camp in the Dark"*.

4th Day. Wednesday September 25, 1878
FOUZILHIC — CHEYLARD L'EVEQUE (breakfast/lunch) — LUC
Overnight at inn in LUC

5th Day. Thursday September 26, 1878
LUC — LA BASTIDE-PUYLAURENT — NOTRE DAME DES NEIGES
Overnight in a room in the monastery of Notre Dame des Neiges

6th Day. Friday September 27, 1878
A late start (pm). Lunched with monks.
NOTRE DAME DES NEIGES — RETURN TO LA BASTIDE-PUYLAURENT
— CHASSERADES
Overnight at inn in Chasseradès.
*"— in the inn kitchen that night were all men employed in survey for one of the
projected railroads."*

7th Day. Saturday September 28, 1878
CHASSERADES — L'ESTAMPE — MONTAGNE DU GOULET — LE
BLEYMARD (lunch) — MONT LOZERE
He camped overnight at 1,400 metres (4,590 feet) on Mont Lozère. *"A Night
among the Pines".*

8th Day. Sunday September 29, 1878
MONT LOZERE — PIC DE FINIELS — PONT DE MONTVERT (lunch) —
TARN VALLEY
Stevenson camped out overnight in the Tarn Valley

9th Day. Monday September 30, 1878
TARN VALLEY — LA VERNEDE (breakfast) — FLORAC (lunch)
Overnight at inn in Florac

10th Day. Tuesday October 1, 1878
"A very late start" ie. after lunch.
FLORAC — TARNON — MIMENTE VALLEY
Camped out overnight in the Mimente valley. *"A little hollow underneath the
oak was my bed"*

11th Day. Wednesday October 2, 1878
MIMENTE VALLEY — CASSAGNAS (lunch) — COL DE LAUPIES — ST
GERMAIN DE CALBERTE
Arrived after dark. Overnight at inn in St Germain de Calberte. *"— I must
have gone supperless to roost."*

12th Day. Thursday October 3, 1878
A very late start: *"—it was long past three before I left St Germain de Calberte."*
ST GERMAIN DE CALBERTE — ST ETIENNE VALLÉE FRANÇAISE — ST
PIERRE — ST JEAN DU GARD

Darkness had fallen by the time he reached the summit of St Pierre. He stayed overnight at the Hotel du Cheval Blanc in St Jean du Gard (now demolished).

Summary of his journey:-

Six nights were spent at inns/*auberges*.
Four nights were spent camping 'wild'.
One night was spent in a room in a monastery.
One night (the last) was spent in an hotel.

APPENDIX FOUR:
USEFUL ADDRESSES

1. French Government Tourist Office. 178 Piccadilly, London W1V OAL Tel (071) 493 3371

2. Edward Stanford Ltd (specialist map shop). 12-14 Long Acre, London WC2E 9LP Tel (071) 836 1321

3. The Map Shop. 15 High Street, Upton-upon Severn, Worcestershire WR8 0HJ

4. Au Vieux Campeur. 48 rue des Ecoles. 75005. Paris. Nearest Metro station: 'Maubert-Mutualité'. Extensive range of French maps and guidebooks.

5. IGN Shop. 107 rue La Boétie. 75008. Paris. Just off the Champs-Elysées. Nearest Metro station: 'Georges V'. Complete range of IGN maps of France at 1:50,000 and 1:25,000.

6. British Airways London Reservation Centre. PO Box 10, Heathrow Airport (London), Hounslow TW6 2JA. Information on relevant flights to the area.

7. National Express Coach Services. Eurolines. Victoria Coach Station, London SW1. Tel (071) 730 0202

8. Thomas Cook Group Ltd. PO Box 36, Thorpe Wood, Peterborough PE3 6SB.
    Tel (0733) 63200. Ask for details of their Independent Traveller Insurance Scheme.

9. West Mercia Insurance Services, High Street, Wombourne, near Wolverhampton WV5 9DN. Tel (0902) 892661. Ask for details of their insurance scheme for 'walking, rambling, scrambling and camping'.

10. Club Cévenol. Mme P.Valette, 6 Avenue Du Mont Aigoual, 30120 Le Vigan, France (send international reply coupon with any enquiries; letters may be written in English).

11. Edinburgh City Library. George IV Bridge, Edinburgh EH1 1EG. Tel (031) 225 5584. A RLS collection is housed in the Edinburgh Room.

12. Chamina *(gîtes d'étape* and rambling in the Massif Central) Maison de la Randonnée Massif Central, 5 rue Pierre-le-Vénérable, 63102, Clermont Ferrand, France.

13. Parc National des Cévennes. Château de Florac. 48400, Florac, France.

BIBLIOGRAPHY

1. *Travels with a Donkey in the Cévennes* by Robert Louis Stevenson. First published in 1879. There have been several versions published including a facsimile copy of the first edition (Godfrey Cave, 1980), a paperback edition (Century Publishing Co.), an illustrated edition (Chatto & Windus, 1986) and combined with *An Inland Voyage* and *The Silverado Squatters* (Everyman Classics). Several of these are now out of print but can usually be obtained from a public library. The continuing popularity of the book will ensure that at least one version of the classic will remain in print in the foreseeable future.

2. *The Cévennes Journal. Notes on a Journey Through The French Highlands* by Robert Louis Stevenson. Edited by Gordon Golding (1978). Mainstream Publishing. The previously unpublished text of the notebooks kept by Stevenson on his 1878 journey, together with later journal additions and other fragments and drawings. This journal formed the basis of *Travels with a Donkey*, published in 1879.

3. *A Village in the Cévennes* by Heather Willings (1979). Victor Gollancz. Describes the traditional way of life in the Cévennes, much of which has now disappeared. Heather Willings wrote the English version of the bilingual centenary guide to the RLS Trail, now out of print.

4. *Walks in Volcano Country* by Alan Castle. Cicerone Press. In preparation. A guidebook detailing two walks in the Auvergne: i) A traverse of the High Auvergne (110 or 160 miles; 10 or 15 days) from Volvic across the Puy de Dôme, Puy de Sancy and Cantal to St Flour and on to Langogne. ii) The Tour of the Velay, a 100 mile (8 day) circular walk around Le Puy, including Mont Mézenc and Meygal.

5. *The Elf Book of Long Walks in France* by Adam Nicolson (1983). Weidenfeld & Nicolson. This 'coffee-table' book contains a chapter (thirty pages) on Stevenson's journey through the Velay and Cévennes, but Florac is omitted, a direct route to Cassagnas being taken from Le Pont de Montvert over the Montagne du Bougès. The chapter is a well written account of the author's walk undertaken during November. The book also contains a chapter on the Auvergne.

6. *Classic Walks in France* by Rob Hunter and David Wickers (1985). Oxford Illustrated Press. Lavishly illustrated with colour and black and white

photographs. A chapter (five pages) is devoted to the RLS Trail. Several other walks in the general region are also featured, including the GR67 (Tour des Cévennes), the GR68 (Tour du Mont Lozère), the GR40 (Tour du Velay) and the GR420 (Tour du Haut Vivarais).

7. *Biographies of RLS*
i) *Robert Louis Stevenson and his World* by David Daiches (1973). Thames and Hudson.
ii) *Robert Louis Stevenson* by Paul Binding (1974). Oxford University Press.
iii) *Robert Louis Stevenson* by James Pope Hennessy (1974). Jonathan Cape.
iv) *RLS: A Life Study* by Jenni Calder (1980). Hamish Hamilton.
Most of these biographies are now out of print but they can be borrowed from a public library. A new biography of RLS by Hunter Davies is to be published in 1994, the centenary of Stevenson's death.

8. *Off the Beaten Track. France.* Edited by Martin Collins (1988). Moorland Publishing Company. Includes chapters on the Cévennes (which contains a section 'In the Steps of Stevenson') and the Ardèche. Written for the adventurous tourist. Good background reading.

9. *Walking in France* by Rob Hunter (1982). Oxford Illustrated Press (hardback) or Hamlyn paperback edition (1983). Useful information on all aspects of walking in France.

10. *Walkers* by Miles Jebb (1986). Constable. Includes a short section on the walking exploits of RLS under the chapter heading 'Tramps'.

11. *Writers' France* by John Ardagh (1989). Hamish Hamilton. A 'coffee-table' style book containing a short account of Stevenson's journey through southern France.

12. *Gîtes d'étape de Randonnée et Refuges, France et Frontières* by Annick and Serge Mouraret. 4th edition (1990). La Cadole. Lists some 3,300 establishments including all those in the Velay, Gévaudan, Ardèche, Vivarais and Cévennes. In French with an English lexicon.

13. *Michelin Green Guides.* Michelin Tyre Company, France.
     i) *Auvergne (including the Bourbonnais).*
     ii) *Gorges du Tarn.*
Both guides are in French. General tourist information.

CICERONE GUIDES

Cicerone publish a wide range of reliable guides to walking and climbing in Britain - and other general interest books

LAKE DISTRICT - General Books
LAKELAND VILLAGES
WORDSWORTH'S DUDDON REVISITED
THE REGATTA MEN
REFLECTIONS ON THE LAKES
OUR CUMBRIA
PETTIE
THE HIGH FELLS OF LAKELAND
CONISTON COPPER A History
LAKELAND - A taste to remember (Recipes)
THE LOST RESORT?
CHRONICLES OF MILNTHORPE
LOST LANCASHIRE

LAKE DISTRICT - Guide Books
CASTLES IN CUMBRIA
WESTMORLAND HERITAGE WALK
IN SEARCH OF WESTMORLAND
CONISTON COPPER MINES
SCRAMBLES IN THE LAKE DISTRICT
MORE SCRAMBLES IN THE LAKE DISTRICT
WINTER CLIMBS IN THE LAKE DISTRICT
WALKS IN SILVERDALE/ARNSIDE
BIRDS OF MORECAMBE BAY
THE EDEN WAY

NORTHERN ENGLAND (outside the Lakes
THE YORKSHIRE DALES A walker's guide
WALKING IN THE SOUTH PENNINES
LAUGHS ALONG THE PENNINE WAY
WALKS IN THE YORKSHIRE DALES (3 VOL)
WALKS TO YORKSHIRE WATERFALLS
NORTH YORK MOORS Walks
THE CLEVELAND WAY & MISSING LINK
DOUGLAS VALLEY WAY
THE RIBBLE WAY
WALKING NORTHERN RAILWAYS EAST
WALKING NORTHERN RAILWAYS WEST
HERITAGE TRAILS IN NW ENGLAND
BIRDWATCHING ON MERSEYSIDE
THE LANCASTER CANAL
FIELD EXCURSIONS IN NW ENGLAND
ROCK CLIMBS LANCASHIRE & NW
THE ISLE OF MAN COASTAL PATH

DERBYSHIRE & EAST MIDLANDS
WHITE PEAK WALKS - 2 Vols
HIGH PEAK WALKS
WHITE PEAK WAY
KINDER LOG
THE VIKING WAY
THE DEVIL'S MILL (Novel)
WHISTLING CLOUGH (Novel)
WALES & WEST MIDLANDS
THE RIDGES OF SNOWDONIA
HILLWALKING IN SNOWDONIA
ASCENT OF SNOWDON
WELSH WINTER CLIMBS
SNOWDONIA WHITE WATER SEA & SURF
SCRAMBLES IN SNOWDONIA
ROCK CLIMBS IN WEST MIDLANDS
THE SHROPSHIRE HILLS A Walker's Guide
SOUTH & SOUTH WEST ENGLAND
WALKS IN KENT
THE WEALDWAY & VANGUARD WAY
SOUTH DOWNS WAY & DOWNS LINK
COTSWOLD WAY
WALKING ON DARTMOOR
SOUTH WEST WAY - 2 Vol
SCOTLAND
SCRAMBLES IN LOCHABER
SCRAMBLES IN SKYE
THE ISLAND OF RHUM
CAIRNGORMS WINTER CLIMBS
WINTER CLIMBS BEN NEVIS & GLENCOE
SCOTTISH RAILWAY WALKS
TORRIDON A Walker's Guide
SKI TOURING IN SCOTLAND

THE MOUNTAINS OF ENGLAND & WALES
VOL 1 WALES
VOL 2 ENGLAND

Also a full range of guidebooks to walking, scrambling, ice-climbing, rock climbing, and other adventurous pursuits in Europe

---

Other guides are constantly being added to the Cicerone List.
Available from bookshops, outdoor equipment shops or direct (send for price list)
from CICERONE, 2 POLICE SQUARE, MILNTHORPE, CUMBRIA, LA7 7PY

CICERONE GUIDES - EUROPE

Cicerone publish a wide range of reliable guides to walking and climbing in Europe, as well as a large selection of guides to Britain

FRANCE
TOUR OF MONT BLANC
CHAMONIX MONT BLANC - A Walking Guide
TOUR OF THE OISANS: GR54
WALKING THE FRENCH ALPS: GR5
THE CORSICAN HIGH LEVEL ROUTE: GR20
THE WAY OF ST JAMES: GR65
THE PYRENEAN TRAIL: GR10
TOUR OF THE QUEYRAS
ROCK CLIMBS IN THE VERDON
THE ROBERT LOUIS STEVENSON TRAIL
WALKS IN VOLCANO COUNTRY

FRANCE / SPAIN
WALKS AND CLIMBS IN THE PYRENEES
ROCK CLIMBS IN THE PYRENEES

SPAIN
WALKS & CLIMBS IN THE PICOS DE EUROPA
WALKING IN MALLORCA
BIRDWATCHING IN MALLORCA
COSTA BLANCA CLIMBS

FRANCE / SWITZERLAND
THE JURA - Walking the High Route and
Winter Ski Traverses

SWITZERLAND
THE ALPINE PASS ROUTE
WALKS IN THE ENGADINE
THE BERNESE ALPS - A Walking Guide
WALKING IN TICINO
THE VALAIS - A Walking Guide

GERMANY / AUSTRIA
THE KALKALPEN TRAVERSE
KLETTERSTEIG - Scrambles
WALKING IN THE BLACK FOREST
MOUNTAIN WALKING IN AUSTRIA
WALKING IN THE SALZKAMMERGUT
KING LUDWIG WAY

ITALY
ALTA VIA - High Level Walkis in the Dolomites
VIA FERRATA - Scrambles in the Dolomites
ITALIAN ROCK - Selected Rock Climbs in
Northern Italy
CLASSIC CLIMBS IN THE DOLOMITES

OTHER AREAS
THE MOUNTAINS OF GREECE - A Walker's
Guide
CRETE: Off the beaten track
Treks & Climbs in the mountains of RHUM &
PETRA, JORDAN
THE ATLAS MOUNTAINS

GENERAL OUTDOOR BOOKS
LANDSCAPE PHOTOGRAPHY
FIRST AID FOR HILLWALKERS
MOUNTAIN WEATHER
MOUNTAINEERING LITERATURE
SKI THE NORDIC WAY
THE ADVENTURE ALTERNATIVE

CANOEING
SNOWDONIA WILD WATER, SEA & SURF
WILDWATER CANOEING
CANOEIST'S GUIDE TO THE NORTH EAST

CARTOON BOOKS
ON FOOT & FINGER
ON MORE FEET & FINGERS
LAUGHS ALONG THE PENNINE WAY

*Also a full range of guidebooks
to walking, scrambling, ice-climbing,
rock climbing, and other adventurous
pursuits in Britain and abroad*

*Other guides are constantly being added to the Cicerone List.
Available from bookshops, outdoor equipment shops or direct (send for price list)
from CICERONE, 2 POLICE SQUARE, MILNTHORPE, CUMBRIA, LA7 7PY*